Great Cycle Routes
The Cotswolds

Jeremy Evans

Great Cycle Routes
The Cotswolds

Jeremy Evans

The Crowood Press

First published in 1997 by
The Crowood Press Ltd
Ramsbury, Marlborough,
Wiltshire SN8 2HR

British Library Cataloguing-in-Publication Data
A catalogue record for this book is available from the British Library.

ISBN 1 86126 030 X

Picture credits
All photographs by Jeremy Evans
Map-drawings by Dave Ayres

Printed and bound by J. W. Arrowsmith Ltd, Bristol

Contents

Introduction

RIDE INFORMATION

Area: Where the ride is located.

OS Map: The relevant OS Landranger 1:50 000 map for the route.

Route: Waymarks from start to finish, with OS grid reference numbers. All of the rides in this book bar the South Downs Way are circular, making it possible to start at a number of locations.

Nearest BR Stations: Most of the routes are accessible from a railway station. Owing to the market-led policies of British Rail which have become extremely bike-unfriendly, it is necessary to check restrictions and costs before you start and board a train.

Approx Length: In miles and kilometres. There should always be some allowance for getting lost or altering the route; so only treat the quoted distances as a rough guide.

Time: This is very difficult to assess, and will depend on factors such as whether the tracks are dry, how many hills have to be climbed, how fast you ride, and how many pubs and places of interest there are en route.

Rating: An 'Easy' ride should be accessible for riders of all abilities, excluding sub-teenage children; a 'Moderate' ride may prove harder in terms of terrain, length, hills, churning those pedals, and possibly navigation; a 'Hard' ride is best suited to experienced offroad riders with a high level of commitment. However these ratings can be changed by the weather – for instance an 'Easy' ride in very dry weather may become a 'Hard' ride when the tracks are churned to mud.

Places to Visit / Top Pubs: Virtually all of these rides feature a number of possible pub stops. I have also indicated cafes and other facilities to enjoy along the route. *NT = National Trust; EH = English Heritage.*

If you wish to hire a bike, a directory of cycle hire outlets is available free from the Cyclists' Touring Club. Send a large SAE to: CTC, 69 Meadrow, Godalming, Surrey, GU7 3HS.

Travel by bike! It's the best way to enjoy Britain's countryside while covering quite long distances, with the option of switching between on-road and off-road to suit the route and conditions.

COMMON SENSE OFFROAD

The tracks and trails used for offroad cycling must be shared. The basic problem for mountain bikers is that bikes are generally so much faster than walkers and horse-riders. That is the principal factor which causes antagonism, but why hurry? Why not take it easy and enjoy the ride? Stick to the following common sense rules, and everyone should be happy.

1. Stay on public bridleways, byways or roads. Never ride on footpaths. Cycling on private tracks or open ground is not usually allowed without permission from the land owner. Always moderate your speed.

2. When you ride offroad, the bridleways and byways are classified as 'Highways'. This means the Highway Code applies, and you can be prosecuted for riding dangerously, especially if you are involved in an accident. Any form of racing is illegal on a public highway, unless it is a specially organized event and permission has been obtained. Byways may also be shared with motorized vehicles. They should give way to cyclists, but as when meeting any vehicle, it is necessary to play safe.

3. Learn how to prevent skids and ride with control to help prevent erosion, especially in the wet. If it is very wet, it is much better to push or carry your bike. Going off the official tracks and trails can cause unnecessary erosion, as well as damaging plant and animal environments.

4. When you meet other people offroad and in the countryside, be courteous and considerate. Always slow right down and give way to both walkers and horse-riders, even if it means dismounting and lifting your bike out of the way. Bikes are almost silent, so give warning of your approach in as polite a manner as possible. The British Horse Society would like you to 'Hail a Horse'; we think the very best policy is to come to a complete halt until the animals have passed you by. If you are riding in a group,

all go to one side of the track. Take particular care when you ride past children – you may not worry them, but you may terrorize/infuriate their parents.

5. Make sure your bike is safe to ride, and won't let you down in the middle of nowhere on a fast downhill – learn basic maintenance and take essential spares. In the interests of safety take drink and food, and wear suitable clothing for the weather conditions and length of ride. It is wise to wear a helmet, putting a layer of polystyrene between your cranium and any hard object in the unlikely event of a bad fall particularly on-road.

6. To avoid getting lost, it is always wise to carry a compass and relevant map such as the OS 1:50, 000 Landranger series. You should know where you are, and have the ability to re-plan the route and cut the ride short.

7. Follow the Country Code. Leave nothing behind – no litter, no orange peel, the minimum of noise, no bad memories for yourself or for others, and if possible not even a sign of your wheeltracks. Always shut gates behind you (unless they should obviously be left open). Don't blast through fields of cows or sheep – neither they nor the farmer will like it. If you ride with a dog for a companion, be sure to keep it under control.

Right: Bridleways are generally well signposted.
You may be able to travel a lot faster than walkers or horseriders who can feel threatened by bikes, so always be prepared to moderate your speed.

USE THAT MAP!

Unless the route is very easy or you know it well, you should never ride without a map, never ride without a compass. Once you get the hang of it, using them is easy and will ensure you know where you're heading.

A map is a diagram which shows the features of an area of land such as mountains, hills, woods, rivers, railways, roads, tracks, towns and buildings. All these and many other features are shown by special signs that map readers can understand. There is always a table on the map which explains the signs. On a 1:50, 000 map (OS Landranger) 1cm on the map equals 50,000cm on the ground; this equals 2cm for every kilometre, or 1¹/₄ in per mile.

THE GRID SYSTEM: Maps are covered by a grid of numbered horizontal and vertical grid lines. The grid is used to find an exact place on a map. To find a grid reference position you read the first three numbers off the vertical grid line which is called the Eastings line. You then read the next three numbers off the horizontal Northings grid line. Where they meet is where you want to be.

CONTOURS: Contours are lines on a map which join areas that are the same height above sea level (in metres). The difference in height between the contour lines is called the vertical height. The closer the lines are the steeper the hill will be. Contour lines are spaced at 10m intervals on 1:50, 000 Landranger maps, and at 5m intervals on 1:25, 000 Outdoor Leisure maps.

It is generally best to arrange your ride so the climbs are short and steep and the descents are long and fast; it is also best to get major climbs out of the way early on the ride. Sometimes it is quite difficult to know if you will be going up or down; a river or stream on the map is a sure sign of dropping down to a valley, but you can also work it out by looking at the contour line height numbers, as the top of the number is always uphill.

USING A COMPASS: A compass is a valuable aid to finding your way. The most popular style is the Swedish-made Silva on which most modern hiking (equally suitable for biking) compasses are based. It is low in price, light, very tough, and easy to use.

The compass should be carried on a lanyard at all times; in bad visibility it may be the only means you have of finding the way. The compass needle always points to Magnetic North, but keep it away from close contact with any metallic object to which it might be sensitive. Knowing that the needle points North, you can always follow a course in the direction you wish to go. The vertical grid lines on a map point to Grid North; this may be a few degrees different from Magnetic North, but the difference is very small.

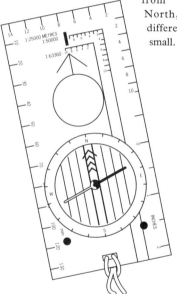

OFFROAD WITH KIDS

Why not take the kids with you? With a little care the whole family can have a great day out, and when the kids are too big for a child seat you can put them in the saddle and still stay in control.

There's no point in taking children cycling on-road or offroad if they don't enjoy it, because then you won't enjoy it. Always follow the three golden rules:

1. Make sure they're comfortable.

2. Keep them amused.

3. Don't bite off more than you can chew.

COMFORT: For a child up to around four years of age, go for the best rear-mounted child seat you can find. It must obviously be secure on the bike, with a high back and sides to help protect its occupant if you should fall, deep footwells to protect the feet, and a full harness to hold the child firmly in; a safety bar for the child to grip on to is also a worthwhile extra. Ideally, the seat should also be quick and easy to put on and take off your bike, so when you ride alone the seat doesn't have to go with you.

It's a good idea to get children used to wearing helmets as early as possible, but with very young children (under one year old) there is a often a problem making the helmet stay on. This results in a miserable baby with a helmet tipped down over its eyes; best then to do without the helmet and be extra careful, until you can be sure it will sit comfortably in position.

Make sure the straps of a helmet are sufficiently tight. Children won't like you fiddling under their chins, and your best policy is to train them to put on and take off the helmet themselves as young as possible, ensuring the straps are adjusted to the right length. Shop around for a child helmet and do ask to try it on. As with most adult helmets, removable rubber pads are used to alter the internal diameter, but the most important consideration is that the design of the helmet and its straps hold it firmly

A child seat works well so long as the child is held in securely and the rider can stay upright; it also acts as a very efficient rear wheel mudguard.

on the head. Some helmets seem to want to slide forward on impact, which is useless.

The child is protected from the headwind by your body, but can still get pretty cold sitting there doing nothing; in winter, an all-in-one waterproof/windproof coverall suit does the job really well. Remember that young children require all sorts of extras – extra clothes, nappies, drink, apples, and so on. Try to keep their requirements down to an acceptable minimum; a neat solution is to carry extras in a small backpack that mounts behind the child seat itself.

KEEP THEM HAPPY: Young children generally love riding on the back of bikes, and want to tell you all about what's going on. It can be bad enough understanding them at the best of

For very young children you can tow a buggy, but this is not recommended on any kind of rough or difficult terrain.

times, but in this situation it becomes ridiculous and your replies degenerate to a meaningless 'Yes' or 'No'.

With that level of conversation a child will only sit happily in its seat for so long; the duration will obviously be affected by the weather, especially if it's freezing and foul. Children like regular stops if they're to stay happy, so take a stash of little treats – apples, nuts and raisins, and so on – and ensure that you get to the picnic or pub (make sure they allow children) on time with the shortest part of the ride left for the end of the day.

Routes should be chosen with care and an eye on safety. A rock-strewn 'downhill extreme', which is just waiting to throw you over the han-

The Trailerbike.

dlebars, should obviously be avoided. To start with, keep to mellow and easy offroad routes such as those found in the New Forest or an old railway line such as the Downs Link in Sussex. Moderate uphills are all right when the weight of the child helps back wheel traction; immoderate uphills are plain stupid, as you wheeze and groan pushing both bike and child together.

What about downhills? As long as you're in control there's no danger in going fast on a smooth track or road. Rather than hitting the brakes, it's better to treat it as a laugh and teach the child to get used to the thrill of safe speed.

There comes a time when children grow too big and bored for a conventional rear-mounted seat, but too young to ride their own bike and keep pace (and keep safe) with adults. One answer is the Trailerbike, a remarkable hybrid, which claims it will take children from four to ten years old with a maximum weight of 42kg (6.5 stone). It allows you to ride with your child; they get all the fun of riding their own bike, but you have total control over their speed, where they go, and ultimately their safety. They can also pedal as much or as little as they like. If they have the muscle and aptitude, they'll help push you uphill as well as down.

OFFROAD RIGHTS OF WAY IN ENGLAND & WALES

PUBLIC BRIDLEWAYS: Open to walkers and horse-riders, and also to cyclists since 1968. This right is not sacrosanct; bike bans are possible if riders are considered to have become too much of a nuisance.

PUBLIC BYWAYS: Usually unsurfaced tracks open to cyclists, walkers, horse-riders and vehicles which have right of access to houses.

PUBLIC FOOTPATHS: No rights to cycle. You probably have the right to push a bike, but the temptation to ride is high and it is best to avoid footpaths whenever possible.

FORESTRY COMMISSION: Access on designated cycle paths, or by permission from the local Forest Manager. At present there is a general presumption in favour of bikes using Forestry land gratis; this may change.

DESIGNATED CYCLE PATHS: Specially built cycle tracks for urban areas; or using Forestry Commission land or railway lines.

Signposts point the way. When you come to a junction, it's wise to check your position on the route before planning the next section.

Official signs like this tend to make good sense, in marked contrast to the vitriolic, hand-daubed 'Get off my land' style notices that one occasionally finds when bridleway pointers are lacking.

PAVEMENTS: Cycling is illegal on pavements. However it is frequently much safer and more pleasant than cycling on the road, and with the proviso that you take great care to avoid pedestrians (who are seldom seen on out-of-town pavements), using pavements can be perfectly reasonable.

13

WHAT IF BRIDLEWAYS AND BYWAYS ARE BLOCKED?

Cyclists are used to being on the defensive on Britain's roads; offroad they should stand up for their rights. The relevant landowner and local authority have the responsibility to maintain bridleways and byways and ensure they are passable with gates that work. It is illegal for a landowner to block a right of way, close or divert it (only the local authority or central government can do this), or put up a misleading notice to deter you from using it.

It is also illegal to plough up or disturb the surface of a right of way unless it is a footpath or bridleway running across a field. In that case the farmer must make good the surface within twenty-four hours or two weeks if it is the first disturbance for a particular crop. A bridleway so restored must have a minimum width of two metres, and its line must be clearly apparent on the ground. A farmer also has a duty to prevent any crops other than grass making a right of way difficult to follow. A bridleway across crops should have a two metre clear width; a field edge bridleway should have a clear width of three metres.

If you run into difficulty on any of the above, you can file a complaint with the Footpaths Officer at the local council, giving full details of the offence and a precise map reference of where it occurred.

Not all bridleways are so perfect. Some are overgrown and impenetrable due to inaction by local authorities; a few are barricaded by selfish land owners who are only slowly being taught the error of their ways.

OFFROAD CARE AND REPAIR

Have you decided on your route, got the right OS map, and your compass? Have you got all the right clothes – ready for rain, wind or sun – plus food and sufficient drink if it's going to be hot? That just leaves your bike, so don't risk getting let down by a breakdown.

BRAKE CHECK: The most important part of your bike – if the brakes fail, you could be dead. Check the blocks for wear, turn them or change them as necessary. Lubricate the cables, check they won't slip, and if there is any sign of fraying, change them. Lube the brake pivots – if the spring return on the brakes isn't working well, they will need to be stripped down and cleaned.

WHEELS: Check your tyres for general wear and side-wall damage; look for thorns. If a wheel is out of line or dented, it needs to be adjusted with a spoke key; also check for loose spokes. Always carry a pump and a puncture repair kit.

CHAIN CARE: Give your chain a regular lube – there are all sorts of fancy spray lubes around, some of which cost a lot of money; however, although the more universal sorts are cheap and reliable, they do attract the dirt. If your chain and cogs are manky, clean them with a rag soaked in spray lubricant or a special 'chain bath'; adjust stiff links with a chain breaker, which is a useful tool to carry.

MOVING PARTS: Clean and lube the derailleur jockey wheels and gear cogs. Lube the freewheel with the bike on its side. Clean and lube the chainwheel gear mechanism. Lube and check the cables for both sets of gears. Lube the bottom bracket – the most basic method is to pour heavy oil down the top tube. Lube the pedals by taking off the end caps. Check that both the cranks and headset are tight. Check that the derailleur lines up properly.

Other things that may go wrong include breaking the chain or having a cable slip, though if you take care of your bike these occurrences

High speed on rough tracks can put a lot of strain on an ill-prepared bike. Make sure you are ready for all eventualities.

are very rare. Just in case, however, it is wise to carry a chainlink extractor, which rejoins a broken chain, 4/5/6mm Allen keys, a small adjustable spanner, and a screwdriver with both a flat head and a Phillips head. The neat solution is a 'multi-tool' which includes all these items in one package.

PUNCTURE REPAIR

The most common offroad repair is a puncture and the most common cause is the hawthorn. To cope with this you need a pump, tyre levers and a puncture repair kit; you may also like to carry a spare tube. Always go for a full-size pump with the correct valve fitting; the pump should fit inside the frame, ideally on the down tube. A double-action pump puts in the air fastest.

Two tyre levers are sufficient, either in plastic or metal, whilst a spare tube saves the hassle of finding the leak and doing a patch offroad – unless you puncture twice.

1. Stop as soon as you feel a tyre go soggy: riding on a flat tyre is asking for trouble. Find a suitable place to do the repair – well away from any cars – and turn the bike upside-down. Take care you know where you put things down: it is too easy to lose that little black screw cap that covers the valve.

2. Undo the brake cable near the brake block, flip off the quick release lever at the hub, and remove the wheel. This is more of a fiddle with the back wheel, and it may be necessary to partly unscrew the hub.

3. You won't get the tube out unless it is well deflated. Carefully insert a lever to get the tyre wall off the rim, and then work the rim off all the way round one side using two levers.

4. Pull the tube out of the tyre. The next thing is to find the puncture. Inflate the tube, and then slowly pass it close to your ear and cheek. You should hear or feel the leak and be able to locate it. If this fails, you can try submerging the tube in a puddle and watch for tell-tale bubbles.

5. When you've found the puncture, keep a finger on it so you don't lose it. Roughen the surrounding area with the 'roughener' provided in your repair kit, and then cover the area

The classic style of puncture repair is time consuming and requires care. A modern option is an instant sticky-back patch, but personal experience shows that it may blow off under very high pressure.

with a patch-sized blob of glue. Now leave the glue to set for at least two minutes.

6. To find out what caused the puncture, run your fingers round the inside of the tyre; the probable cause is a thorn which is still in the tyre. Remove it carefully.

7. The glue should now be set enough to put on the patch which should bond straight to the tube. If it seems OK, partly inflate the tube, which makes things easier when getting the tyre back onto the rim.

8. Reassemble the wheel and put it back on the bike. Connecting the brake cable first ensures the wheel is centred by a pull on the brake lever before you tighten the quick release hub; it also ensures you don't ride off with the brake undone. Now inflate the tyre fully.

SAFETY OFFROAD

The first rule of offroad touring is to allow enough time. Getting caught by nightfall is foolhardy and potentially dangerous, particularly if the ride ends in an on-road section and you have no lights. So before you leave, work out how much time to allow, and be pessimistic. Your speed will depend on your skill, level of fitness, and the riding conditions.

Tackling a route after heavy rain in midwinter may take three times as long as the same route in dry summer weather. Riding along a disused railway line will be fast and easy; riding up and down big hills can be exceptionally demanding, and the difference in speed between a good and not so good rider will be much greater.

Riding in a group should ensure some degree of safety, but groups which are much bigger than three riders bring their own problems. They can put an unacceptable load on other people's enjoyment of the environment; walkers and horseriders were there first, and while they can cope with small groups of bike riders, it's no fun for them when a dozen or so Tour de France lookalikes blast through their favourite countryside. By contrast riding alone has much to recommend it; you cause minimum upset to others, and also don't have to worry about keeping up with the fastest member of the group, while the slowest rider doesn't have to worry about keeping up with you.

Whether you ride alone or in a small group, before leaving the golden rule is *tell someone:*
- When you're going.
- When you expect to be back.
- Give them some idea of your route.

It doesn't happen often, but riders do occasionally fall off and knock themselves out or break a few bones in the middle of nowhere; if that happened to you, it would be nice to know that someone would come looking for you, and that they'd be able to locate you before too long.

A First Aid kit is only of value if someone knows how to use it, and even then the constrictions of space and weight on a bike will make its application limited; some bandages and plasters will be enough to deal with minor cuts and abrasions, or possibly support a fracture. In most cases injuries from falls are fairly minor, and you can keep on riding; in more serious cases it will probably be a case of getting help ASAP, while caring for the injured rider:
- If two crash, help the worst injured first.
- If a rider is unconscious, don't leave him on his back. Use the First Aid 'recovery position' if you know how, and cover him with a coat if possible. If a rider is unconscious and not breathing, give the kiss of life if you know how.
- Staunch any bleeding by applying a pad or hand pressure; if bleeding is in an arm or leg, raise the injured limb unless broken.
- Don't move the rider if he seems to be paralysed, unless in immediate danger.
- Don't give the rider anything to eat, drink or smoke.
- Don't leave the injured rider alone.

If you ride regularly it's well worth attending a full length course to get a First Aid certificate which is valid for three years. These are run all round the UK by organizations such as the British Red Cross Society, whose phone number can be found in the local telephone directory.

Keep off areas like this, and offroad riding is potentially as safe as any sporting pastime can be.

The Cotswolds

Bounded by Stratford, Evesham, Cheltenham, Gloucester, Stroud, Bath, Cirencester and Witney, the hills of the Cotswolds and their neighbouring flatlands offer a huge choice of routes for the intrepid cyclist. The area is laced with a massive network of bridleways and quiet country lanes that tie together the famous towns and villages that are so well known for their mellow Cotswold stone buildings. Stow-on-the-Wold, Chipping Campden, Bourton-on-the-Water and Winchcombe are among the best known on any tourist itinerary, but the rides that follow will take you deeper into the mystery of the Cotswolds as you visit the places where car-borne, road-dedicated travellers simply cannot go.

I enjoyed the research and riding that went into these routes as much as any other area I have ridden in Britain. With the proviso that you should pick your weather to avoid the mud which is a well known bike-disabling Cotswold distraction, with this 25 route selection there are plenty of guaranteed great rides for you to follow.

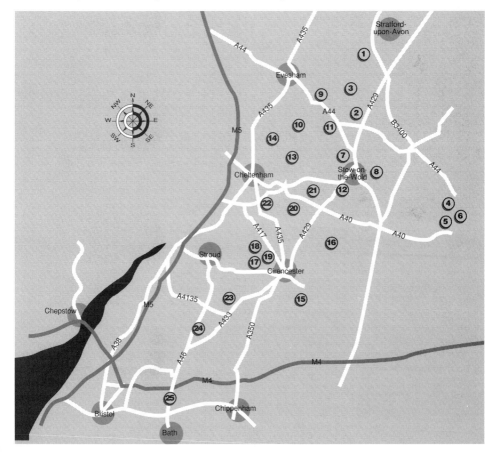

19

1 A Stratford Circuit

On-Road and Offroad

Area: South of Stratford-upon-Avon to the northern fringes of the Cotswolds. Start and finish at Stratford-upon-Avon by the Royal Shakespeare Theatre at GR:205547.

OS Maps: Landranger 151 – Stratford-upon-Avon & surrounding area.

Route:
Stratford-upon-Avon (GR:205547)
River Avon/Avon Valley Cycle Path/bridleway (GR:188533)
Long Marston (GR:153479)
Lower Quinton (GR:183471)
Ilmington/bridleway (GR:214440)
Newbold-on-Stour (GR:247462)
Armscote (GR:247449)
Halford/bridleway (GR:259455)
Ettington Park/bridleway (GR:252473)
Shennington/A422 (GR:249506)
Loxley (GR:259530)
Stratford-upon-Avon (GR:205547)

Nearest BR Station:
Stratford-upon-Avon.

Nearest Youth Hostel: Stratford-upon-Avon (tel: 01789 297093).

Approx Length: 27 miles (43.5km).

Time: Allow 3 hours plus stops.

Rating: Easy. Most of the going is pretty easy with little in the way of hills, but in wet weather mud could slow you down.

Stratford-upon-Avon is within easy reach of the north fringes of the Cotswolds, and this circuit out of the Bard's own town provides a pleasant tour of the surrounding countryside. The terrain is mainly flat, but there is enough variety to make the route enjoyable.

1. Start from the Royal Shakespeare Theatre on the north bank of the River Avon. There are a number of car parks nearby, but be aware that Stratford gets very busy in the main tourist season, when a car will prove a liability.

From the Royal Shakespeare Theatre head west along the road beside the river, and then turn right up into the town and follow the signs for the A4390 and Newbold-on-Stour. This leads you to a roundabout on the south fringes of the town from where the Avon Valley Cycle Route is signposted.

2. The Cycle Route follows an old railway line on a good hard surface, heading south-west past the race course to cross the River Avon. It then bears south past the smelly sewage works and Milcote Manor Farm, before coming to the road at Weston where it continues straight on until it eventually reaches a dead end by the depot at Long Marston some 5¹/₂ miles (9km) out of Stratford. So far it's easy, pleasant cycling all the way.

3. Turn left on the road at the end of the old railway line, riding west to cross the B4362, and continue through Lower Quinton. Here you can turn south on a very minor road that passes below the local high point of Meon Hill, bearing west again to ride into Ilmington. This part of the route is along quiet country lanes, with the slightest of hill climbs to add some interest.

4. Bear left to join the main road at Ilmington, turning right signposted for Armscote and Halford, and then immediately take the first farm drive on the left, which heads north below the overhead power lines and is an unsignposted bridleway.

Continue along a good track by the side of

A Stratford Circuit

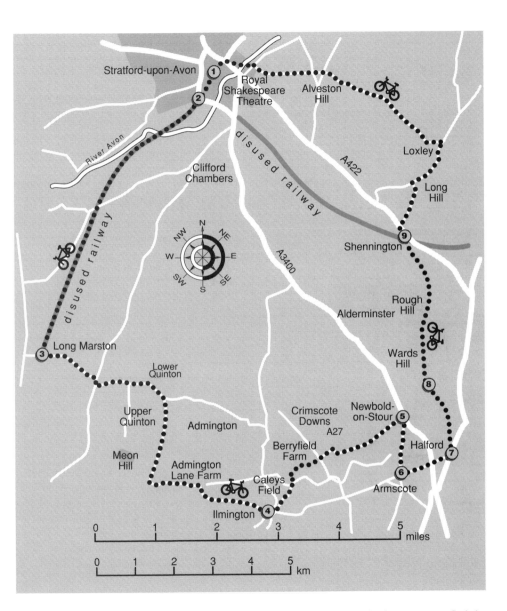

Caleys Fields, bearing left and then right round the side of a copse of trees – don't take the track into the trees here, which comes to a dead end.

The bridleway track continues past an isolated barn to the south of Berryfield Farm, crossing an unsurfaced farm lane to continue along the side of a strip of woodland where you may find the riding muddy after wet weather. Not far on, the track turns right and left through the woodland, joining a track with a better surface that crosses open country to bring you to the main A3400 at Newbold-on-Stour.

5. The direct route from here is to follow the A3400 south, but it's more pleasant to follow a dog-leg diversion along the minor road that goes due south towards Armscote.

6. At the first junction turn left to head east, crossing straight over the main A3400 and following the signpost for Halford. As you drop down the hill, keep left to follow the old road, which is now closed to traffic as it crosses the old river bridge. Keep well away from the new bridge that supports the traffic on the main A429.

7. Ride on up past the pub in Halford, then take the first narrow left turning which heads into the hidden heart of the village, passing close by the church to join a bridleway that starts on a track by the side of a cottage.

In early spring the first part of the bridleway is an avenue of daffodils, leading you down to a gate set in a belt of trees, from where the bridleway heads due north by the side of the River Stour. It's a well signposted and easily followed route, with the riding pretty easy as the bridleway leaves the river to join a fine track that speeds you northwards between two mighty oaks.

8. At the Ettington Park Hotel the track bears right on a slight uphill, after which the bridleway turns right and left to continue away from the hotel, going due north through woodland and crossing a lane at Ward's Hill. The next section up Rough Hill is a little more up and down with a surface scattered with the debris of felled trees. You might suffer from mud here in wet weather, but things improve as the route breasts the top of Rough Hill. Less than 1,000yd (1km) further on the main track bears left, but the bridleway carries straight on along a clearly marked narrower track. This will speed you down to join a country lane a few metres short of the main A422 at Shennington.

9. From here it would be great if you could follow the old railway line back into Stratford,

but the deep cutting is totally overgrown and is clearly a very suitable case for Sustrans. Until the hoped-for happy day when the railway route opens, it's road all the way back to Stratford. If you don't mind stretching the route to avoid the A422, the reward is a pleasant enough way to finish any ride.

10. Turn left onto the A422 at Shennington, then take the first right signposted to Loxley. The climb up the side of Long Hill is probably the stiffest of the whole route, but from there on it's almost all downhill with the pub at Loxley offering a pleasant diversion.

From Loxley turn west to follow the old country road back into Stratford with easy ups-and-downs between fields. On the outskirts of Stratford you will need to negotiate the confusing one-way system, crossing the River Avon by the old bridge. From here a left turn takes you past the busy junction of the Stratford Canal, finishing the ride in plenty of time for a Royal Shakespeare Company performance, with a seat in the Swan Theatre my recommendation for Elizabethan dramatophiles.

Places To Visit:
Information Centre (tel: 01789 293127) at Stratford-upon-Avon;
The Royal Shakespeare Theatre (tel: 01789 295623) and various Shakespeariana including Shakespeare's Birthplace, Anne Hathaway's Cottage and Mary Arden's House at Stratford-upon-Avon.

Pubs and Cafés:
The Howard Arms at Ilmington; wide choice of everything in Stratford.

2 Moreton-in-Marsh to Chipping Campden

On-Road and Offroad

Area: Between Moreton-in-Marsh and Chipping Campden in the north of the Cotswolds. Start and finish at Moreton-in-Marsh at GR:206327; alternatively start from Chipping Campden at GR:153393.

OS Maps: Landranger 151 – Stratford-upon-Avon & surrounding area.

Route:
Moreton-in-Marsh (GR:206327).
Batsford Park/bridleway (GR:188339)
Blockley (GR:164348)
Dovedale/bridleway (GR:162345)
Holt Farm/bridleway (GR:146355)
B4081/bridleway (GR:143370)
Broad Campden (GR:158378)
Chipping Campden (GR:153393)
Broad Campden (GR:158378)
Paxford (GR:184379)
Draycott (GR:183360)
Aston Magna (GR:198358)
Batsford Park (GR:188339)
Moreton-in-Marsh (GR:206327)

Nearest BR Station:
Moreton-in-Marsh.

Nearest Youth Hostel: Stow-on-the-Wold (tel: 01451 830497).

Approx Length: 18½ miles (30km).

Time: Allow 3 hours plus stops.

Rating: Moderate. A few ups and downs add a little physical interest to what is otherwise an easy ride.

Moreton-in-Marsh is one of the most pleasant Cotswold market towns with the added advantage of a main line railway station. The route that follows gives a good tour of the area to the north-west, and can be linked to Chipping Campden and the route that follows (Ride 3) to form a double circuit. Alternatively the ride can be started from Chipping Campden.

1. From the car park near the Moreton-in-Marsh railway station, turn right onto the main street and follow it northwards. Just before the railway bridge, take the left turn by a pub to join a narrow lane signposted to Batsford. This takes you straight into pretty countryside, with the beginnings of an uphill as you come close to Batsford Park.

2. At Batsford Park it's worth a diversion to see what little there is of the charming hamlet of Batsford with its church and dramatic stable block, and an arboretum and falconry centre shrouded by trees. From here continue to follow the road north-west along the side of Batsford Park, with a steep climb up to the top of Cadley Hill.

3. At the top of Cadley Hill go straight ahead where the road bends sharp left. Here you join a signposted bridleway by a field gate, following the field edge along the top with good views opening out over the valley below.

The bridleway route becomes a little confusing as you reach a patch of trees on the hillside; take the signposted direction below the woodland, passing through a field that on my visit claimed to be home to a presumably friendly but unseen bull. From here you drop down the hill, passing behind a new barn to join a hard track which soon brings you to the village of Blockley with a slight uphill as you come to the road.

4. The straightforward route through Blockley is to turn right via the pub and church, and then turn left to follow the dead-end lane which heads south-west towards Dovedale.

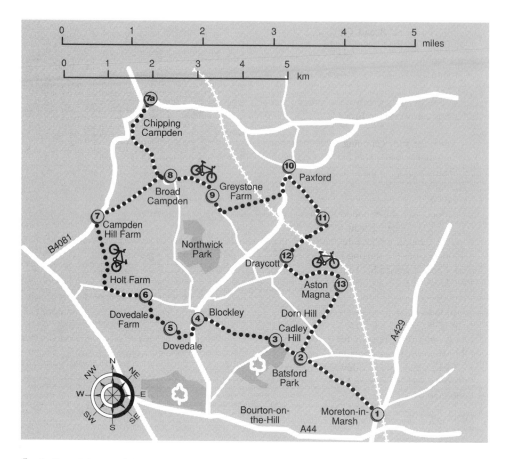

5. At Dovedale turn right uphill by the side of a cottage to follow a narrow dead-end lane that leads straight to a bridleway going north-west. From here a steady but quite easy uphill along the side of a field brings you to Dovedale Farm where you turn through the farmyard, joining the farm track that leads out to the road due west of Blockley.

6. Turn left along the road from Dovedale Farm, and follow it for approximately two-thirds of a mile (1km) westwards along the top of the ridge. Turn off when you come to a driveway/track on the right heading downhill to the Northwick Hill Estate. This is an unsignposted bridleway, which has a fast surface that takes you quickly down into the forested valley. Here you ignore tracks off to the right and left, keeping straight on up the hillside. Turn left at the top, following the bridleway away from the farm barn with its 'No Right Of Way' sign, and then ride on through a belt of trees to follow the bridleway round the side of fields en route to the B4081. Once out of the woods the direction of travel stays much the same on all this section, and with reasonable bridleway signposting it's easy enough to follow.

7. From the B4081 junction the quickest way to the honeypot town of Chipping Campden is to follow the B4081 on a long downhill. However it's much more fun to take in an offroad diversion via Broad Campden. Turn right along the B4081 for a very short distance, and then turn right off it onto the wide track signposted to the Northwick Quarry. This gravel bridleway section soon leads onto a narrow track that bumps you speedily downhill into the valley, giving a great ride to Broad Campden.

7a. To connect with Chipping Camden from Broad Campden, turn left and follow the road for approximately two-thirds of a mile (1km). Look out for a bridleway sign on the right as the road bends left by a few houses at Westington. Take this turn, and follow the narrow lane past the playing fields, bearing right to ride into the east end of Chipping Campden close by the entrance to the old Banqueting Hall. The same route can be recommended to re-connect with Broad Campden.

8. From Broad Campden follow the road eastwards as it wiggles its way past the rather good pub. Just past the turn-off for the original Quaker Meeting House, bear left onto a very narrow lane which swoops downhill then up; then take the next left turn to head east following the signpost for Paxford.

9. Less than a mile (about 1km) out of Broad Campden this quiet road starts a long downhill. Past the entrance to Greystone Farm look out for a bridleway sign on the left, which will lead directly across the flatlands to Paxford. The bridleway follows the side of a field – expect mud here in wet weather – and then crosses the railway line, where there are dire warnings concerning suitable punishment for those foolish enough to leave the gates open. From here keep straight on for Paxford, reaching the outskirts of the village and the road by a large house on the left.

10. Follow a loop round the north side of Paxford, passing the pub before bearing southeast on a narrow lane that heads towards the old Upper Dutchford Village. Then just under a mile (about 1km) out of Paxford look for a

The view across to Batsford Park before starting the first big hill of the day.

bridleway track signposted on the right.

11. This bridleway follows a good track along field edges, recrossing the railway under a bridge and after a few twists and turns eventually reaching the road at Draycott. On the plain beneath the down it's flat country and easy riding all the way.

12. Turn left onto the road and be prepared for a stiff uphill all the way to Aston Magna where you need to look out for the narrow right turn just as the road starts to go downhill.

13. Follow this lane over the top of Dorn Hill and back to the Batsford crossroads, from where it's an easy ride back into Moreton-in-Marsh.

Places To Visit:
Information Centre at Chipping Campden (tel: 01386 840101); Batsford Park Arboretum (tel: 01608 650722).

Pubs and Cafés:
Baker's Arms at Broad Campden; The Crown Inn at Blockley; wide choice of pubs and cafés in Chipping Campden; The White Hart or Redesdale Arms in Moreton-in-Marsh.

3 Chipping Campden High Tour

On-Road and Offroad

Area: The top of the Cotswolds –
a circuit exploring the hills to the north
of Chipping Campden. Start and finish
at the Dover's Hill car park to the north-
west of Chipping Campden at
GR:137397; alternatively start and finish
from the centre of Chipping Campden at
GR:153393.

OS Map: Landranger 151 – Stratford-
upon-Avon & surrounding area.

Route:
Dover's Hill CP/bridleway (GR:137937)
B4035 (GR:144409)
Burnt Norton/Middle Norton bridleway
(GR:151416)
Mickleton/bridleway (GR:162436)
Kiftsgate Court/Hidcote Manor junction
(GR:173430)
Nebsworth/bridleway (GR:196427)
Windmill Hill/bridleway (GR:207423)
Ebrington (GR:188401)
Chipping Campden (GR:153393)
Dover's Hill CP (GR:137937)

Nearest BR Station:
Moreton-in-Marsh.

Nearest Youth Hostel: Stow-on-the-
Wold (tel: 01451 830497).

Approx Length: 15 miles (24km).

Time: Allow 3 hours plus stops.

Rating: Moderate. There are some
good hills and long offroad sections.

*This is a very fine circuit on the hills above
Chipping Campden, which lays claim to
being the most beautiful small town in the
Cotswolds. The Dover's Hill car park, a
short way to the north-west of the town,
makes a good place to start from; alternatively you can start from the centre of
Chipping Campden itself, where you have
the option of linking the route with Ride 2,
which extends south to Moreton-in-Marsh.*

1. From the Dover's Hill car park look north-
east, and go through the bridleway gate on the
right side by the trees to follow a route which
will soon get you away from the car-borne walkers who are up there for the view. Follow the
bridleway signs by the side of the trees, passing
close to the trig point and then joining a track
which winds through woodland and steeply
down to a gate. Continue to follow the bridleway in a north-east direction – it's easy riding on
the hillside but there could be mud – until you
come down to the B4035.

2. Turn right along the B4035, which is a fairly quiet road, and then take the first left on the
B4081 signposted to Mickleton. A short way on
take the left turning 'private road' bridleway to
Attlepin Farm, and continue to the top of the
hill where it bears left downhill to the estate at
Burnt Norton. Here the bridleway leaves the
drive to bear off downhill through parkland to
the right, heading through a couple of gates and
across fields at the bottom where it may be
muddy after rain.

3. Keep on towards Middle Norton Farm,
crossing the driveway and then following a track
across the grassland. This bears left on a slight
uphill away from the farm buildings, leading along
the side of a field to the B4632, which it joins at
Dairy Hills between Broadway and Mickleton.

4. Turn right on the B4632, crossing over the
railway and then riding on to bear left into
Mickleton, which is a prosperous-looking
village. Ride through the village until you

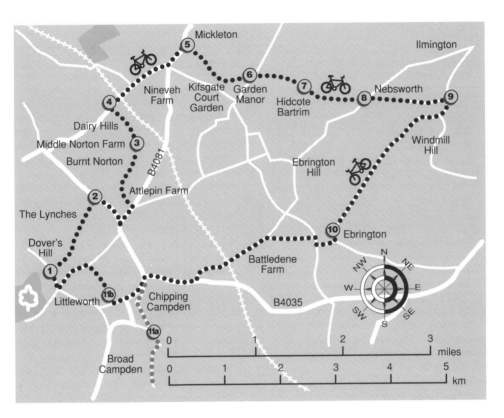

reach the church backing onto the fine manor house, and turn right up the dead-end lane by the side of the church. Take care, as a few heavy lorries rumble along this otherwise quiet section of the route.

5. The lane leads round the churchyard, bearing left to come up to an old steel fence with a bridleway gate. Go through here and cross the meadow ahead, keeping to the right and going through the next gate in the far right corner.

The bridleway continues straight ahead with the choice of a narrow track going through the middle of a belt of trees, or keeping to a track that follows the field edge on the left. At the next gate the track starts on a steady uphill, which brings you beneath Kiftsgate Court, a fine house with gardens that are a magnificent sight in spring. Keep on following the faint track to the

final uphill to the road – this is very steep but in dry conditions should be ridable all the way.

6. At the top of the hill you come out on the road by the entrance to Kiftsgate Court. Cross straight over here, and follow the lane ahead to continue riding due east. This leads you past the entrance of Hidcote Manor and its equally fine gardens, and in season you are bound to encounter a steady stream of cars going to and from the Hidcote car park. Ride on past them and join a rough track which is bridleway leading you on a steady uphill.

7. From Hidcote the track leads up to a high point by the 259m trig point, winding round the side of open fields before coming to a conspicuous radio installation by the side of a lane. Cross straight over on the high ground here, fol-

27

The small town of Chipping Campden is notable for its wonderful buildings. This is the view at stage 11a.

lowing the track straight ahead, and then downhill through woodland to the next lane, which it meets close to the Downs House on the hillside.

8. Turn left and almost immediately right at this lane, joining a track that climbs up to the tall radio masts on the top of the hill at Nebsworth. From here the track keeps straight on due east, with a few lumps and bumps on the way as it starts to head downhill by the side of woodland before coming out to the next lane about a thousand yards (1km) south of Ilmington.

9. Turn right here to head south, and where the road bends left bear right to follow a private tarmac driveway which is bridleway, going straight ahead. This gives a fast ride on a steady downhill towards the huge mansion at Foxcote, a most magnificent pile in its own hidden valley. Follow the drive round the right side of the house and then downhill to a gate, which leads you up past the farm buildings. Here the hard driveway tarmac comes to an end and you join a track that continues south-west across the fields. It dips and dives on a slight downhill to cross a steam, climbing back up to join a straight, fast track that eventually becomes full tarmac as it leads into the hamlet of Ebrington.

10. Turn right onto the road at Ebrington, following the signs for Chipping Campden which is about 1³/₄ miles (3km) distant.

11a. From Chipping Campden you can divert to Broad Campden to join Ride 2 to Moreton-in-Marsh. Keep left past the big church on the outskirts of Chipping Campden and ride on past the fine entrance to the East Banqueting House. After 50yd take the first lane on the left which connects to a bridleway passing the recreation ground, which leads out to the road to the north-west of Broad Campden.

11b. To continue direct from Chipping Campden to Dover's Hill, ride on past the Banqueting Hall entrance and almshouses and bear left down the busy main street, passing the old marketplace.

Some way on, take the first right turn by a church which is signposted as the Cotswold Way. Head up past a few modern houses, joining a track that goes quite steeply up the hill. The bridleway and footpath are separated here, with the bridleway well broken up by horses and likely to be a nightmare in wet weather. At the top of the hill turn left along the road, and then take the first right turn to the Dover's Hill car park.

> ***Places To Visit:***
> Information Centre (tel: 01386 840101) in Chipping Campden;
> Woolstaplers Hall Museum (tel: 01386 840101) in Chipping Campden;
> Kiftsgate Court Gardens (tel: 01386 438777);
> Hidcote Manor and Garden (NT – tel: 01386 438333).
>
> ***Pubs and Cafés:***
> Pubs and cafes at Chipping Campden;
> Baker's Arms at Broad Campden (off route).

4 North of Charlbury

*The extended village of Charlbury is a good
centre for offroad riding on the mainly flat
countryside which lies to the immediate
east of the Cotswolds, and has the benefit of
a handy youth hostel very close to the
tracks. This ride is recommended by
Oxfordshire County Council, who produce a
number of leaflets outlining suitable routes.
The going is easy and navigation is
straightforward.*

1. From the large car park in the centre of
Charlbury, find your way onto the B4022,
which heads north for Enstone. As the road
starts to head downhill on the outskirts of this
overgrown 'dormitory' village, look out for the
track on the right with a bridleway sign which
leads along Clarke's Bottom.

2. Follow this track on an easy surface as it
breaks out between fields, keeping straight on
for over a mile (about 2km) until you come to a
T-junction crossing track with the way ahead
barred by a thicket of trees. Turn left here and
follow the bridleway track for more than 1³/₄
miles (3km) to the north-west.

3. Keep on past an isolated cottage at
Norman's Grove, passing a hidden trig point
and watching for the right-turning track that
leads on past a dilapidated caravan by the
side of Shilcott Wood. If you get it wrong and
follow the more obvious track to the left, you
will need to turn right on the B4022 road
ahead. If you get it right, you cross straight over
as the bridleway continues in the same north-
west direction. Watch for the traffic which can
come hurtling over a blind hill here.

Follow the track ahead on a good surface
for another mile (1.5km) until you reach a wide
sweep of the B4026 on a bend.

4. Follow the road straight ahead to Chalford
Green, keeping left at the B4026 turn-off to join
a lane that runs due west across the flat countryside. Ignore the first track to Galleypot Farm
on the left, and then just past East Downs

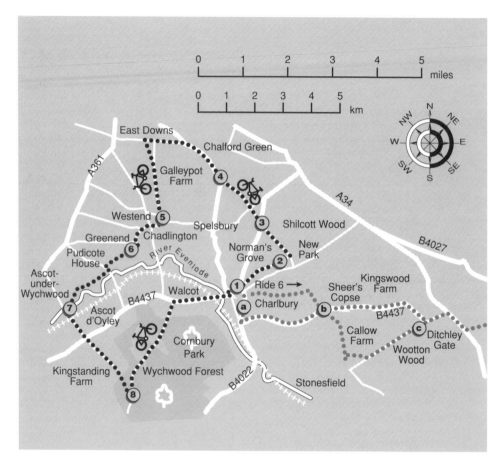

Farm, which is on the right, take the clearly signposted bridleway track that heads south along the edges of the fields. This gives about 1³/₄ miles (3km) of offroad riding to Chadlington, with a slight downhill and a good hard surface all the way.

5. In Chadlington turn right – or left for the pub – to head into Westend, riding straight over at the crossroads to join a minor road by Brookend, where a left turn takes you south for a short distance.

As the road swings west on a left-hand bend, turn onto a lane on the left that leads to the farm at Greenend. A short way on, turn

right through the green painted field gate as shown by the bridleway sign here, ignoring the footpath that continues straight ahead.

6. From Greenend a track loops round a rather fine ornamental pond, following the side of fields with the possibility of a certain amount of mud en route to the next road junction, which is at a quiet lane opposite the entrance to Pudlicote House. Turn left for a short downhill here, and then turn right at the first signpost showing part of the Oxfordshire Way. This takes you through gates and across grassland with plenty of sheep on the way.

There is one slightly confusing section

Easy hills characterize this part of the Cotswolds where there is just enough roll in the land to make the views interesting.

where the bridleway signs appear to direct you down to the River Evenlode, although the sensible option is to follow the clear ridge that goes ahead on the high ground. This leads onto a clear track where you pick up another bridleway sign, crossing the River Evenlode on a wide bridge and coming to the outbuildings of the old Manor House on the outskirts of Ascott-under-Wychwood. Turn right here, and then go left over the railway level crossing and ride into the village.

7. Keep straight ahead through Ascott-under-Wychwood, passing the school before a steady uphill takes you south-east out of the village and up to a road junction. Cross over onto the bridleway that leads straight ahead, starting as a tarmac lane to Kingstanding Farm. Further on it turns to an unsurfaced track, swooping and looping on a fast downhill to join the road on the south-west fringes of Wychwood Forest at Hatching Hill.

8. From Hatching Hill it would be so nice if you could find a forest trail to get you back to Charlbury via Cornbury Park. Despite plenty of tracks running through the woods on the OS map there appears to be no right of way, and instead you and your bike will have to follow the quiet road along the fringes of the forest. This is agreeable enough riding, eventually reaching the B4437 with a fine, final downhill to lead you over the railway and river and then steeply uphill into Charlbury.

Places To Visit:
Blenheim Palace at Woodstock (tel: 01993 811325) to the south-east of Charlbury;
Cogges Farm Museum near Witney (tel: 01993 772602) south of Charlbury.

Pubs and Cafés:
Choice of pubs in Charlbury;
The Tite Inn at Chadlington.

---

5 South of Charlbury

**On-Road
and Offroad**

Area: East of the Cotswolds between
Chipping Norton and Witney – a tour
of the countryside south of Charlbury.
Start and finish at Charlbury at
GR:360198.

OS Maps: Landranger 164 – Oxford
& surrounding area.

Route:
Charlbury (GR:360198)
Walcot/bridleway (GR:347197)
Shorthampton/bridleway (GR:329200)
Chilson/bridleway (GR:319195)
Ascott-under-Wychwood (GR:301188)
Farfield Corner/bridleway (GR:305162)
Potter's Hill (GR:298153)
Fordwells (GR:309139)
Leafield/bridleway (GR:323154)
Singe Wood/bridleway (GR:350142)
North Leigh (GR:386131)
Ashford Mill/bridleway (GR:385155)
East End/bridleway (GR:396151)
Stonesfield/bridleway (GR:393170)
Charlbury (GR:360198)

Nearest BR Station: Charlbury,
Ascott-under-Wychwood.

Nearest Youth Hostel: Charlbury (tel:
01608 810202).

Approx Length: 22 miles (36km).

Time: Allow 3 hours plus stops.

Rating: Moderate. The going is fairly
easy, but it's a good distance.

*This is the number one ride out of
Charlbury, giving a fine tour of the countryside, which offers mostly easy riding with
plenty of good tracks and trails along the
way. To extend the length it can be mixed
and matched to fit in with Rides 4 and 6,
giving a very full tour of the area.*

1. From the centre of Charlbury head downhill to cross the river on the B4437, following
the same outward route as Ride 4. Just past the
railway station look for a track on the right leading to Walcot, and follow it past a few houses to
join the bridleway track that continues west to
the road near Shorthampton. The track follows
field borders with a few ups and downs along
the way.

2. Turn right onto the road, and then almost
immediately left towards the dead-end hamlet of
Shorthampton. Here you follow the Oxfordshire
Way as bridleway, going straight ahead across
more fields and then joining a hard track that
leads to the road at Chilson.

From here the Oxfordshire Way bridleway
continues with a left and a right turn by the
church, as it zigs and zags along an easily followed route to reach a lane at Ascott d'Oyley.
Follow this lane round to the left and straight on
to Ascott-under-Wychwood, where you rejoin
the route of Ride 4.

3. Turn left uphill to leave Ascott-under-
Wychwood, riding up to the junction of the
B4437 where you turn right to head south-west
for a short distance. Then fork left to follow a
lane that heads due south for about 1 1/4 miles
(2km) to the crossroads at Farfield Corner.

4. Go straight over at the Farfield Corner
crossroads. From here on the OS map shows a
bridleway going south and west via the radio
establishment at Langley, but the reality is that
it is a restricted tarmac road all the way and you
are likely to meet a few cars. The next junction
comes just over 2/3 mile (1km) further on at
Potter's Hill.

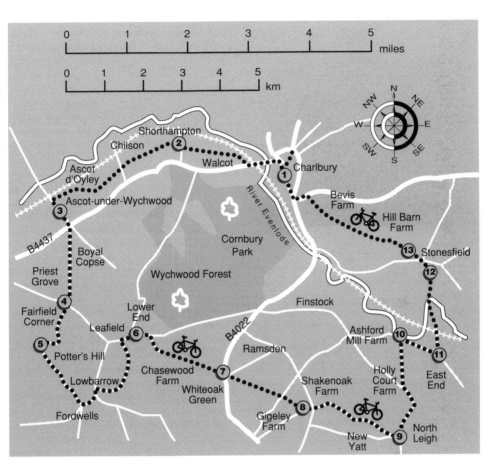

5. Turn left to head downhill on the minor road here, entering the pretty hamlet of Fordwells, where you can pause by the old well. Then bear left uphill and follow the minor roads that lead through the village of Leafield.

6. Ride eastwards through Leafield, and past the pub look out for a lane turning off to the right by the last buildings.

This lane leads south to a few isolated houses, turning to a bridleway track by the last thatched house. It continues through woodland on a dead straight track that must once have been a Roman road, and while the woodland offers very pretty surroundings with the smell of

wild garlic all around in spring, you should beware of mud.

7. Keep straight ahead at the B4022 road crossing close by Whiteoak Green. Follow the bridleway on fairly good tracks as it continues dead straight by the side of Singe Wood, joining a narrow lane to head on past Gigley Farm and then bearing left to a crossroads.

8. From the crossroads a 'white road' continues straight ahead and is signposted as bridleway. Ignore the left turning to Shakenoak Farm and the right turnings to New Yat, following the track as it winds on through a small stretch of

Many sections of the Oxfordshire Way are bridleway, providing an important offroad route for cycles.

woodland – more mud can be expected here – and into the village of North Leigh.

9. Turn left through North Leigh, and follow the road northwards to the next T-junction where you turn left again to head downhill. Ride on for about ¹/₄ mile (0.5km), looking out for a signposted bridleway track on the right that leads down behind Holly Oak Farm. Ignore the tracks that turn right and go up into the woods, and follow the bridleway straight ahead by the side of the stream here, using a narrow track with a good surface that brings you back to the road close to Ashford Mill after about ²/₃ mile (1km).

10. The bridleway emerges on the south side of the crossroads by Ashford Mill on the banks of the River Evenlode – not on the east side as shown on the OS map. Turn right before the road bridge to keep on the south side of the river, and head fairly steeply uphill, climbing high above the river with woodland on both sides before breaking into open country on the road that leads on towards East End.

11. About ²/₃ mile (1km) from the crossroads, look out for a track that leads left downhill

before the next mass of woodland. As well as being bridleway, this is signposted to a Roman Villa administered by English Heritage.

Follow the bridleway down a fast, bumpy track, diverting to inspect the remains of the villa if you have the inclination – it would make a nice spot for a picnic. Otherwise carry straight on to cross over the railway line, shutting gates as you go.

Leave the main track as signposted by the bridleway markers to continue north across the fields, crossing the River Evenlode at a narrow bridge where horses are expected to ford the water. From here the bridleway leads fairly steeply uphill into the village of Stonesfield, climbing on a narrow track that is badly eroded and will require the occasional dismount.

12. Turn left past the church in Stonesfield, heading north on the road towards the next church where there a short bridleway section that cuts the corner. This is formed by a narrow tarmac track that goes down between the houses and is easily missed. If you overshoot, you can simply turn left at the next road junction.

13. Join the bridleway track that goes straight ahead and is signposted as part of the Oxfordshire Way. Follow it on a hard gravel surface past the first farmstead, and from there keep following the Oxfordshire Way signposts to ride north-westwards back to Charlbury. The tracks are mainly good, following the sides of fields with a few ups and downs, and after some 1³/₄ miles (3km) of enjoyable offroad riding they bring you to the B4437 from where it's a swift pedal back into the centre of Charlbury.

Places To Visit:
Blenheim Palace at Woodstock
(tel: 01993 811325) to the south-east
of Charlbury.

Pubs and Cafés:
The Bell or The Bull in Charlbury.

6 North of Woodstock

On-road and Offroad

Area: East of the Cotswolds and Charlbury – a big bridleway circuit north of Woodstock. Start and finish at Charlbury at GR:360198; alternatively start from the centre of Woodstock at GR:446168.

OS Map: Landranger 164 – Oxford & surrounding area.

Route:
Charlbury (GR:360198)
Dustfield Farm/bridleway (GR:381200)
Stonesfield/bridleway (GR:403177)
Ditchley Gate (GR:423189)
Oxfordshire Way/A34 (GR:436186)
B4027/bridleway (GR:453188)
Woodstock (GR:360198)
B4027/bridleway (GR:453188)
Upper Dornford Farm/bridleway (GR:458216)
Whistlow/B4030 (GR:453257)
Brasenose Farm/A423 (GR:463263)
Steeple Aston (GR:477260)
Lower Heyford/bridleway (GR:491248)
Northbrook/bridleway (GR:490220)
Kirtlington/bridleway (GR:499199)
Pound Hill (GR:478193)
B4027/A4095/bridleway (GR:474184)
Woodstock (GR:360198)

Nearest BR Station: Heyford or Charlbury.

Nearest Youth Hostel: Charlbury (tel: 01608 810202).

Approx Length: 19 miles (30km) for Woodstock circuit; 34 miles (55km) including Charlbury.

Time: Allow 3 hours plus stops for Woodstock circuit; allow 1½ hours to ride to and from Charlbury.

Rating: Moderate. Fine if it's dry, but could be grim if it's been wet. Best left for high summer.

This ride is centred on Woodstock with its magnificent Blenheim Palace. It is within easy reach of Oxford with a route connection to Charlbury that allows it to be tacked onto the Cotswold rides. The offroad sections are very pleasant if it is truly dry, but can be diabolical if it has been wet with the heaviest, clingiest, messiest mud you can imagine. You have been warned! Either start the ride from the centre of Woodstock, or from Charlbury, where the route can be combined with Rides 4 and 5.

From Charlbury:

A. This connecting route avoids using roads as much as possible and is consequently less direct. Ride up through the town and past the youth hostel, turning left by a phone box along Ditchley Park Road for a short distance before forking right onto a clearly signposted bridleway. This leads due east on a good track across flatlands, before following the sides of fields to the isolated settlement at Dustfield Farm. There is no bridleway signposting here, but the route turns right to head south along a wide grass track with 1km of easy riding bringing you to the B4437.

B. Cross straight over the B4437 and keep left on the bridleway, which is easily followed downhill past a very large house on the fringes of Sheer's Copse, and from there on down and back uphill to join a hard track which leads out to a lane close by Callow Farm. Turn right here and then take the next signposted bridleway

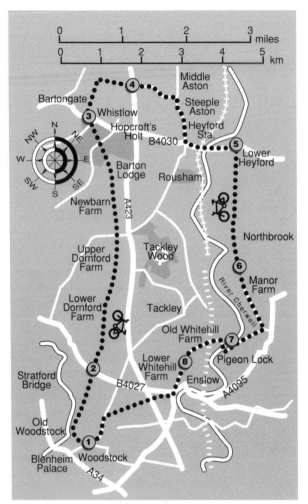

most of the minor roads, and then go left as you come close to the A34 to follow a part of the Oxfordshire Way eastwards across the River Glyme at the Stratford Bridge. This leads out to the B4027 south of Wootton. Turn right past a strangely sited theatre centre on the corner, and after 100yd look out for a signposted bridleway track on the left which puts you on the Woodstock circuit about 1¼ miles (2km) north of Woodstock at the start of Section 2.

From Woodstock:

1. From the Information Centre in the middle of Woodstock turn left onto the main street that leads north-east towards Tackley. Take the first left turning after the church on the left, joining the perimeter road on the northern fringes of Woodstock and then bearing right onto a dead-end road that leads into a bridleway. This passes the cemetery and the sewage works before joining a narrow track that runs through trees by the side of the River Glyme. A mainly good surface and a few mild ups and downs lead on to the B4027 road junction where you can link the route with Charlbury.

2. From the B4027 the bridleway track takes you north for around 4½ miles (7km) of offroad riding. It is easily followed through mainly quiet surroundings, but in wet weather some of the sections can be horrendous.

Keep on along a steady uphill track between trees, breaking out into the open to cross the farmland of Upper Dornford and Newbarn Farm, before the track eventually leads down and uphill into the very smart grounds of Barton Abbey, which has been

track on the left, riding past a very modern looking mansion on the outskirts of Stonesfield to join a long, straight road. This leads past Wootton Wood to Ditchley Gate, where it joins the B4437 on the fringes of Blenheim Great Park.

C. From Ditchley Gate ride on along the B4437 and cross the fiendish A34 with great care, taking the signposted direction for Wootton. Take the first right turn to make the

turned into a hotel. Ride on past the Abbey rooftops – the rest is hidden by the hillside – and out to the road at Whistlow.

3. If you want to cut the ride a little shorter at this stage, you can simply turn right along the B4030 for Lower Heyford. If you prefer to extend the ride a short way north, take a left and a right turn to find the bridleway track which heads northwards across fields, with little in the way of signposting until you reach the 90 degree right turn that will take you eastwards to the A423 at Brasenose Farm – if you reach the trig point, you've overshot the turn.

4. Cross the A423 with great care, following a lane ahead into Steeple Aston, and then turning south by the church to reach the bridge over the River Cherwell, which is controlled by traffic lights. Cross the river, railway line and Oxford canal, heading uphill through Lower Heyford and looking for the bridleway sign on the right, which is just before you come to the next main road junction.

5. The bridleway from Lower Heyford heads due south across fields. The first part is not particularly easy to follow, and the mud here can be horrendous. Keep on south and you will join a hard track for a while, before crossing more fields and then coming close to a fine bridge by a bend in the Oxford canal. This is by the old farm buildings at Northbrook where an alternative bridleway crosses the canal into Tackley.

6. From Northbrook keep on heading south along the side of fields, until you reach the splendours of Manor Farm, where smart gates and a hard driveway bring you quickly to the outskirts of Kirtlington. When you reach the green, turn right onto a potholed track that will take with westwards and downhill to Pigeon Lock by the side of the Oxford canal.

7. At Pigeon Lock you can cross the canal by a narrow bridge, with a somewhat complex route leading on across the river. The OS map shows the bridleway turning right through the grounds of the big house by the canal side, but locals told me it has not gone that way for at least twenty years and now follows the route signposted as 'Footpath' along a potentially mud-churned track. Once over the river, keep left and follow a hard track under the railway and onto the road at Pound Hill.

8. Turn left at Pound Hill and ride as far as the B4027/A4095 junction, crossing over and bearing right onto a narrow bridleway track that heads through shrubby woodland before breaking out into open ground towards Woodstock. For much of the distance this bridleway follows a line of hedges and trees down the centre of fields, which is not that easy riding and is dire in wet weather. However, it's only 1¼ miles (2km) to the road, where you turn left for Woodstock and coast into this bustling tourist centre, which despite the crowds retains a certain amount of charm.

Return to Charlbury:
Either retrace the outward route with your own offroad variations, which could take in the Oxfordshire Way west from Stonesfield, or take the direct road route, following the B4437 all the way back into Charlbury. This offers around 4½ miles (7km) of fairly pleasant riding with easy ups and downs, and the road is wide enough to coexist in reasonable harmony with passing cars.

Places To Visit:
Information Centre at Woodstock
(tel: 01993 811038);
Blenheim Palace (tel: 01993 811325)
at Woodstock.

Pubs and Cafés:
All kinds of pubs and cafés at
Woodstock, where the Feathers is
worth investigating;
The King's Head at Wootton;
The Bell or The Bull in Charlbury.

7 Stow-on-the-Wold Circuit

**On-Road
and Offroad**

Area: The north-east Cotswolds – a ride heading west out of Stow-on-the-Wold. Start and finish at Stow-on-the-Wold at GR:195257.

OS Maps: Landranger 163 – Cheltenham & Cirencester area.

Route:
Stow-on-the-Wold (GR:195257)
Maugersbury (GR:200252)
A429/A424/bridleway (GR:190243)
Lower Swell (GR:176253)
Lower Slaughter (GR:164225)
Upper Slaughter/bridleway (GR:153232)
Eyford Park/bridleway (GR:146245)
Chalk Hill (GR:132260)
Ryknild Street/bridleway (GR:157261)
Condicote (GR:150281)
Longborough (GR:180296)
Donnington (GR:193283)
Broadwell (GR:204274)
Stow-on-the-Wold (GR:195257)

Nearest BR Station:
Moreton-in-Marsh.

Nearest Youth Hostel: Stow-on-the-Wold (tel: 01451 830497).

Approx Length: 19 miles (30km).

Time: Allow 3 hours plus stops.

Rating: Moderate. This is steady country with no big hills and fairly easy navigation.

Stow-on-the-Wold is one of the finest Cotswold towns and a personal favourite. In the main square you will find the perfectly placed youth hostel, with a free car park on the southern outskirts of Stow just off the A436, which makes a good place to start this ride if you have arrived by car. The route takes in a few classic Cotswold locations on the way, and has the advantage of being ridable in wet weather.

1. Turn right out of the car park on the south side of Stow, and follow the road south-east to Maugersbury which is about 500yd (0.5km) distant. At the phone box bear right through this hamlet, joining the dead-end lane which heads west past the Manor.

2. This is the old road, which has been cut off at the A429 and now provides very pleasant, hassle-free riding. Keep on past the Manor, continuing to follow the old road along the side of the valley until you come out to the anti-car barriers at the A429 less than a mile (about 1km) south of Stow-on-the-Wold by St. Edward's Well.

3. The A429 is quite busy with cars and lorries. The least stressful option is to turn left down the pavement, and where the road splits into the A424 and A429 (the old Foss Way) cross straight over using the traffic islands. You can then join a tarmac driveway close by a hotel, which is signposted as bridleway.

4. Follow the drive straight ahead here, passing a few houses and eventually coming to the imposing entrance to the house at Hyde Mill. There is no bridleway sign, but this is the correct way to go, following the driveway round the right side of the house and over the River Dikler. Here you come to a bridleway sign pointing right to Lower Swell and a footpath signs pointing left to Lower Slaughter.

5. Stick to the bridleway and bear right through a gate, climbing up the side of a mead-

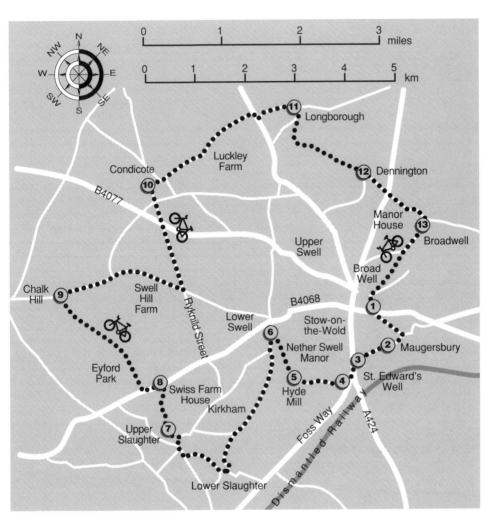

ow and along by the side of a wire fence to join a track that leads up into the hamlet of Lower Swell. Here you can turn right to visit the pub, or turn left to continue to the ride towards Lower Slaughter.

6. Fork left and follow the ups-and-downs of this quiet lane southwards for just over 1¾ miles (3km) into Lower Slaughter, which is one of the ultimate Cotswold picture-postcard villages. Bear left past the church here, and then

immediately turn right along the side of the River Eye which passes in front of the classy-looking hotel and a fine terrace of houses. Ride out of the village to follow the road for less than a mile (about 1km) to the sister village of Upper Slaughter, which is rather less picturesque but equally impressive.

7. Turn right downhill into Upper Slaughter as signposted, crossing the River Eye, and immediately turning left onto the loop lane, which leads round to the church. Recross the river, and just below the church turn right onto a clearly signposted bridleway track that follows the hillside by the side of the river and offers wonderful riding through beautiful woodland.

The track then breaks out of the woods to follow the river northwards, bearing left past the attractive Swiss Farm House on the facing hillside to emerge on the B4068 at the foot of a hill.

8. Turn left on the B4068, and after a short distance uphill turn right by the side of some estate cottages onto the tarmac driveway that leads north-west towards the big house at Eyford Park. Follow the driveway behind the big house, and when you come to a small cottage by a field gate join the bridleway which takes over as a track. Follow this straight on through Eyford Hill Farm to join the road at Chalk Hill, which is a fast ride all the way.

9. Turn right on the road here, and follow it eastwards towards Stow-on-the Wold. After 1¼ miles (2km) you will pass Swell Hill Farm on the right; take the next left track which is part of Ryknild Street, an old Roman road heading north-to-south and marked as unsuitable for vehicles. It gives great riding for bikes, though if it's been wet the puddles can be deep. Keep straight on to cross the next two roads and join a tarmac lane leading into the hamlet of Condicote.

10. Bear right through Condicote, and follow the road for just over 1¾ miles (3km) to Longborough, taking care with the right and left turn needed to get across the busy A424. Turn right at the foot of the hill by the school in the middle of Longborough (there's a handy pub in the village), and follow the road south until you come to the green with a gushing water pipe (in winter), which gives a brilliant free bike wash if it's been muddy.

11. Keep left downhill from the green, following a narrow lane past a dead-end sign to join a

bridleway track by a field gate. Ride on across a lowland meadow, and then follow the bridleway on a narrow track uphill through trees, with a sharp left turn leading to a section that can be ferociously muddy. At the next gate you break out of the trees, but there is no signpost showing which way to go; bear over to the right, and you will find a gate at the top of the hill with a track leading on round the front of the big house on the outskirts of Donnington, where a bridleway sign directs you onto the driveway.

12. Turn left here to follow the lane south-east across the busy A429, keeping left downhill into the village of Broadwell. Past the fine Victorian church take the first right turn on a left-hand bend (or continue straight on to the pub), and follow this narrow lane round the back of Broadwell to a patch of houses on a green, where you take the next right turn on a slight uphill.

13. Follow this lane south-west out of Broadwell, passing a large estate on the left and then coming to a narrow track set in woodland on the left, which is signposted as footpath though shown as bridleway on the OS map. This conveniently cuts the corner off the A429, leading south-west to join a lane at Stow Well on the outskirts of Stow-on-the Wold and a short ride from the start point.

Places To Visit:
Information Centre at Stow-on-the-Wold (tel: 01451 831082).
The Old Mill at Lower Slaughter (tel: 01451 820052) boasts an ice cream parlour and tea room.

Pubs and Cafés:
Lots of choice in Stow-on-the-Wold where the Queen's Head can be recommended;
The Five Bells at Broadwell.

8 Stow to Shipton

**On-Road
and Offroad**

Area: The north-east Cotswolds – a ride connecting Stow-on-the-Wold with Shipton-under-Wychwood using bridleways and quiet lanes. Start and finish at Stow-on-the Wold at GR:195257; alternatively start from Shipton-under-Wychwood at GR:278181.

OS Maps: Landranger 163 – Cheltenham & Cirencester area.

Route:
Stow-on-the-Wold (GR:195257)
Maugersbury/bridleway (GR:200252)
Icomb (GR:213229)
Nether Westcote (GR:227202)
Fifield/bridleway (GR:240187)
Shipton-under-Wychwood (GR:278181)
Bruern Abbey/bridleway (GR:263203)
Foscot (GR:250221)
Bledington/B4450/bridleway
(GR:243230)
Lower Oddington (GR:232259)
B4450 (GR:219250)
Maugersbury (GR:200252)
Stow-on-the-Wold (GR:195257)

Nearest BR Station: Shipton-under-Wychwood.

Nearest Youth Hostel: Stow-on-the-Wold (tel: 01451 830497).

Approx Length: 35km (22 miles).

Time: Allow 4 hours plus stops.

Rating: Moderate. Very little in the way of hills; a few problems with navigation; watch out for mud!

This ride goes from Stow-on-the-Wold as far as Shipton-under-Wychwood and offers a variety of terrain and conditions. There are a few hills, none of which are particularly taxing, but when you hit the flatlands north of Shipton you should beware of mud after wet weather when following the course of the River Evenlode on the return leg. The ride shares the same start point as Ride 7 and could be combined into a big tour of the area.

1. From the main Stow-on-the-Wold car park, just off the A436, turn right and ride down to Maugersbury. Here you go straight ahead up a dead-end lane by the phone box, which leads steeply downhill to a bridleway.

2. Follow the bridleway due south on a good track, crossing the river and riding on through the farmyard at Oxleaze Farm, where it may become muddy. From here, there's a steady climb up Maugersbury Hill, with the track continuing straight on to emerge by a lane at the top of Icomb Hill. Bear left to ride down into Icomb, which is a well-heeled hamlet approached via narrow lanes.

3. From Icomb there are two possible routes to connect with Nether Westcote to the south. The most direct way is to follow the road west and then south to join the A424 for a short distance, taking the first turn-off to the east where a lane leads via the attractive hamlet of Church Westcote to Nether Westcote.

3a. The alternative is an offroad route that may present some problems. Follow the lanes east from Icomb, and then at Pebbly Hill farm turn right onto a clearly signposted bridleway that starts by following a hard track due south past the equestrian centre. This track soon deteriorates, and in wet weather turns into the most fearful muddy mess, which will totally clog up your bike. The worst section is where a hoof-churned track runs between high hedges with no escape to either side, before the route crosses

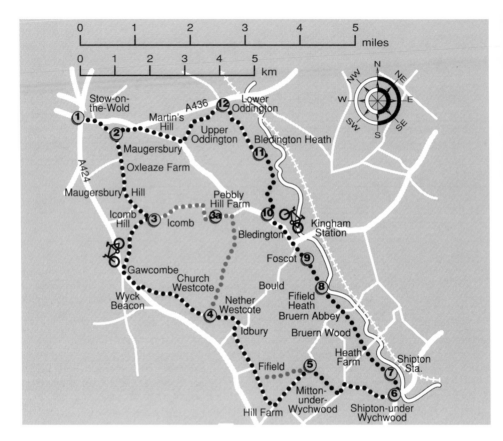

the Westcote Brook to continue along the side of fields. The bridleway signposting is non-existent here, and I ended up joining the track that leads up to Nether Westcote, which is rough, ripped and likely to be horribly muddy in wet weather. The track that leads direct to Nether Westcote may or may not be a better option.

4. Follow the road from Nether Westcote east to Idbury and from there south to Fifield. Just past this hamlet you can take a bridleway that leads across the fields to cut the corner, or stay on the road as it's all quiet, pleasant riding here, and take the next left turn at Hill Farm to link up the route.

5. Just past the farmyard of Grange Farm,

which is on the left, look out for a signposted bridleway track leading off to the right. This takes you though an orchard, and then across fields to the small town of Shipton-under-Wychwood where you turn left at the road.

6. Ride on through Shipton-under-Wychwood for almost 1¼ miles (2km). Turn left onto the A361 Chipping Norton road, and then take the first turn-off to the left before you reach the river.

It's signposted as part of the Oxfordshire Way. Follow this dead-end road northwards past a few houses on the outskirts of Shipton, joining a track which leads out to a field. Here the footpath goes straight on to cross the river at a bridge, while the bridleway – which is also part of the Oxfordshire Way – bears left round the side of the field and then crosses the field on a raised section which is bumpy riding though the open countryside is pleasant enough.

7. Continue to follow the Oxfordshire Way bridleway as it heads north-west on a 3³/₄ miles (5km) long section. The going gets better as it heads across more fields, crossing a lane by Heath Farm and then heading into Bruern Wood, where you ride down an avenue of trees that leads straight to the very fine building ahead, which is Bruern Abbey. This is now a school, and the bridleway cuts between the buildings and the cricket pitch, bearing left to cross a lane and then following a narrow track through pretty woodland, which can, however, be a muddy turmoil in wet weather.

8. Less than a mile (about 1km) past Bruern Abbey there is a bridleway sign pointing right across the river. However, the correct route goes straight on ahead, and if it's muddy you may do better to join the dead-end road that runs parallel to the left, connecting the small group of houses at Foxholes with the hamlet of Foscot.

9. Having reached Foscot by bridleway or road, turn right and left through Foscot to join the B4450, which leads directly back to Stow-on-the-Wold. However, if you're game for it, there's more offroading as you ride through Bledington.

10. On the outskirts of Bledington, just beyond the pub, the offroad option can be recommended when conditions are dry. Turn off to the right onto the hard track, which is signposted as bridleway, and follow it to bear right into the woods. From here on you are in bad trouble if there has been plenty of rain as the track is mightily churned by tractors and can boast some of the most horrific puddles known to man or beast! Keep on following the track north – it's easy navigation even if the surface leaves much to be desired.

The view across to Bruern Abbey. It's fine, flat cycling for much of the distance here, but dry weather is necessary to make the route really enjoyable.

11. For a time the track improves as it enters the woodland at Bledington Heath, but if it's been raining you'll also be entering a remarkable area where you can expect to get wet up past your knees. In dry weather it could be a lovely ride through the woods, eventually bringing you to a hard track that leads to the church of Lower Oddington, where there's a potential pub stop.

12. Turn left to head west from Lower Oddington, and follow the country lane through Upper Oddington for the last pub stop, and onto the B4450. Here there's a steep climb up Martin's Hill, with a left turn taking you downhill and uphill into Maugersbury, following a quiet lane, which is a better option than entering Stow on the main A436.

Places To Visit:
Information Centre at Stow-on-the-Wold (tel: 01451831082).

Pubs and Cafés:
Lots of choice in Stow-on-the-Wold, where the Queen's Head can be recommended;
The Shaven Crown or Lamb Inn at Shipton-under-Wychwood;
The King's Head at Bledington.

9 Round Broadway

This is a fine tour of the country surrounding Broadway offering at least three options for start points – either from Broadway itself, from the hamlet of Snowshill, which is most convenient for linking with Rides 10 and 11, or from the large free car park at Tilbury Hollow on the A44 to the east of Broadway. The latter is probably the best option for those arriving by car and the one we will take as our start point.

1. Turn right out of the Tilbury Hollow car park, and cross straight over the A44 with care – it is a grim road, much beloved by high-speed motorists. Go straight onto the narrow lane ahead, passing through the fine entrance gates to the Broadway Tower. Keep straight on to the Tower itself, which is well worth a visit and the price of the climb to the top. Then carry on southwards along the quiet lanes, and follow the signposts down to Snowshill.

1a. An alternative bridleway route is enjoyable but misses out on the Broadway Tower. From the A44 at Tilbury Hollow turn left along the A44 for no more than 200yd, and then cross over to join a track as indicated by a bridleway sign. Keep through the right-hand gate, and follow a good surface up and down along the side of fields, leading due south to a lane. Turn right past Seven Wells here to reconnect with the route at Snowshill.

2. Ride downhill past Snowshill Manor (NT and well worth a visit – check out the amazing Japanese armour) with the pretty little church on your left side. Follow the narrow lane ahead as it starts a steep uphill passing a strange Gothic garage on the left, and a track that is signposted as footpath on the right. Keep on up to the top of the hill, and then as the lane bears left go straight ahead – with due care – onto a tarmac track that leads to the west.

3. This track passes a solitary house in a fine position on the right before it splits into two. Take the right fork here to turn northwards, and

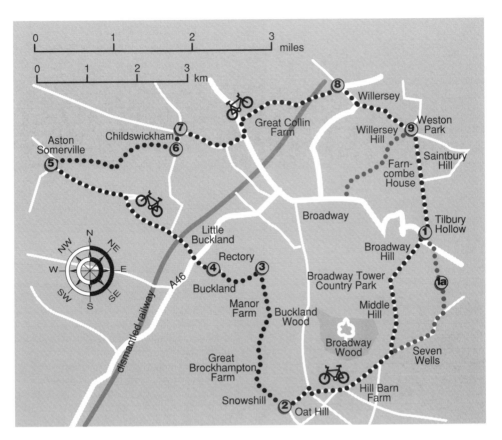

follow the track along the hillside contours past Great Brockhampton Farm. This is a lovely ride with fine views out of the valley. Keep straight on as the tarmac is left behind, with a good surface speeding you on to Buckland Wood, where the surface gets considerably rougher as the track drops downhill past Manor Farm.

Continue to follow this track through gates, rejoining a tarmac surface to speed steeply down to the hamlet of Buckland in the next valley – watch out for the tight hairpin on the way down.

4. From Buckland follow the road out to the A46. Cross straight over to follow a long, quiet lane for just over 1³/₄ miles (3km) into the village of Aston Somerville. Turn right at the T-junction by the bus shelter here – a good place to stop and check the map – and ride on to where the road bends sharp left. Here you turn right as shown by a bridleway sign pointing eastwards.

5. This starts as a good track heading east with an alternative bridleway turning off to the north. The eastbound bridleway follows the side of fields, and can soon become horribly, cloggingly muddy in wet weather. If you encounter such conditions you are advised to pick up your bike and carry it without delay before the mud gets a stranglehold. Rest assured there are no more problems of this kind along the route.

Keep on following the bridleway as it bears north round the side of a field, eventually

45

Snowshill is a lovely little place and worth some time for the Manor, the Snowshill Arms and the seasonal café opposite.

joining a hard track by a barn and emerging at a lane close to a market garden on the outskirts of Childswickham.

6. Turn left into the village of Childswickham, and then right at the crossroads by the pub on the corner. This road will take you directly into Broadway if you want to pay this well known tourist-trap a visit. Alternatively, look out for a bridleway track turning off to the left after about 200yd. This leads between fields on a good surface, passing a dilapidated barn and then going past a modern house where on my visit two fearsome dogs were thankfully chained in position. Follow the hard track that continues up to the A44.

7. Cross the A44 with care and turn right. You will probably prefer to ride on the pavement as far as the next left turning, from where it's a gentle ride eastwards through flat country towards Willersey, crossing a disused railway, which, like so many, would make a fine cycle track.

8. At Willersey turn right for a short distance along the A46, bearing left as the road bends sharp right by a church. This leads you up a narrow lane going eastwards, which soon starts to head steeply up Willersley Hill, so steeply that it's a challenge to ride all the way to the top. At least this road tends to be more or less car-free along the way, however, and the surroundings are very pleasant.

9. Near the top of Willersey Hill you come to a crossroads by Weston Park. Turn right to follow the road south for 1¼ miles (2km) back to the start point at the Tilbury Hollow/A44 car park, or alternatively turn off onto the signposted bridleway that leads all the way back down into Broadway.

Places To Visit:
Information Centre at Broadway
(tel: 01386 852937). Attractions include Broadway Tower and Country Park (tel: 01386 852390) and Snowshill Manor (NT – tel: 01386 852410).

Pubs and Cafés:
Plenty of choice in Broadway. At Snowshill the Snowshill Arms is in a very pleasant setting and there is an excellent seasonal cafe across the road.

10 Snowshill to Hailes Abbey

On-Road and Offroad

Area: The north of the Cotswolds – a tour of the hills and high ground to the south of Snowshill. Start and finish at Snowshill at GR:098337.

OS Maps: Landranger 150 – Worcester, the Malverns & surrounding area.

Route:
Snowshill (GR:098337)
Cotswold Way/bridleway (GR:083341)
Stanway Ash Wood (GR:084322)
Stumps Cross/bridleway (GR:077303)
Bridleway/road (GR:066280)
Farmcote/bridleway (GR:062290)
Hailes Abbey (GR:050300)
A46 (GR:045310)
Stanway/B4077 (GR:061322)
Stanton/bridleway (GR:067341)
Shenberrow Hill/bridleway (GR:080333)
Cotswold Way/bridleway (GR:083341)
Snowshill (GR:098337)

Nearest BR Station: Evesham.

Nearest Youth Hostel: Stow-on-the-Wold (tel: 01451 830497).

Approx Length: 15¹/₂ miles (25km).

Time: Allow 2–3 hours plus stops.

Rating: Moderate. Be prepared for a good climb up Shenbarrow Hill.

This is a great ride south from the hamlet of Snowshill, where there's a car park on the Broadway road leading north out of the hamlet. Snowshill is a lovely little place, and Snowshill Manor has to be one of the best National Trust houses in the land – look out for the super spooky room full of Japanese samurai and then forget about them in the neighbouring pub! The route also links with Rides 9 and 11, which are based on the same area.

1. From the Snowshill car park, bear right downhill through the village, with Snowshill Manor on your right and the church to the left. Keep on straight up the short steep hill ahead, and at the top where it bends right go straight ahead on a tarmac track following the same route as Ride 11.

2. Past the last solitary house on the right take the left fork to keep heading west on a steady uphill. The track then bears north on a very good surface, and after less than a mile (about 1km) leads up to bridleway crossroads by a quarry. This is signposted as part of the Cotswold Way, running due north to south.

3. Turn left through the field gate to head south along the Cotswold Way here. The track follows the top of the ridge along the edge of fields and is mainly good riding, though you have to open and close plenty of gates along the way and can expect big puddles after rain. In just under 1¹/₄ miles (2km) it brings you down to a quiet lane at Stanway Ash Wood.

4. Turn right here and follow the lane south, going straight over at the next road junction, and keeping straight on for just over 1¹/₄ miles (2km) to Stumps Cross. Here you reach the B4077, where you will see the bridleway continuing directly opposite. This leads past the farmstead at Upper Coscombe, and on for about 1¹/₂ miles (2.5km) to an isolated road junction 2¹/₂ miles (4km) to the west of Winchcombe, offering good riding all the way.

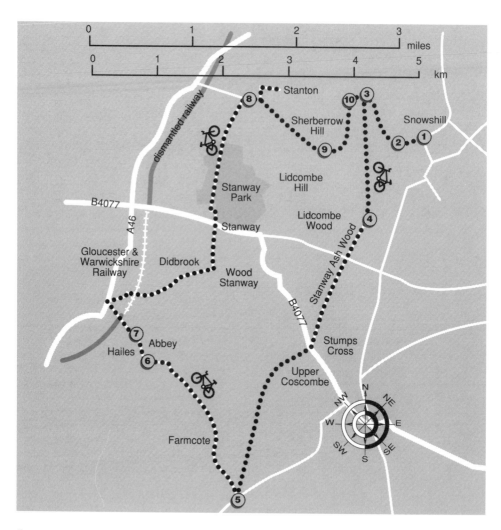

5. At the road junction turn right to follow the direction signposted as a dead-end road to Farmcote. This narrow lane leads up and down along the side of the valley, passing the magnificent small manor house at Farmcote and then continuing past a couple of very smart farmhouses to join a track that is bridleway even though it lacks a signpost.

Keep on down the rough but easily ridable track, passing through the southern fringes of Hailes Wood with fine views over the valley. As

you emerge from Hailes Wood at the bottom of the hill, look out for the fruit farm, farm shop and café signposted to the left, which is worth a visit to stock up on provisions or stop for a cup of tea. From there ride on along the quiet lane, soon reaching Hailes Abbey on the left.

6. Hailes Abbey is a very fine monastic ruin with a small museum. It is well worth the admission price for anyone interested in old architecture, and with several benches

The ruins of Hailes Abbey are well worth a look, and if the weather is fine enough it's a good place for an impromptu picnic.

strategically placed inside the ruins, it is also an excellent place for a picnic before moving onto the next stage.

7. From Hailes Abbey ride on westward to the A46, and then immediately turn right to head east on a minor road signposted to Didbrook – take care with this manoeuvre. Cross the railway and ride on through Didbrook, bearing north to cross the B4077 by a fine memorial that signals the start of Stanway Park. Keep on riding north, passing the front of Stanway House, which is a most magnificent pile, and heading for Stanton some 1¹/₄ miles (2km) distant.

8. Keep right in the hamlet of Stanton, where you will find the pub improbably situated on the eastern fringes of this attractive village at the top of a short, steep, dead-end hill. The bridleway that leads up over the hill to Snowshill is some way back along the road, on the apex of the first sharp left hand bend as you enter Stanton from the south. It heads uphill across rough fields, climbing Shenberrow Hill on a surface that can be cattle churned and too difficult to ride, though as compensation the scenery is very fine.

9. Near the top of Shenbarrow Hill the track enters a belt of trees and the riding becomes

much easier as you pass the back of a large farmstead on the hilltop. Here you join a hard farm track that speeds you due north to rejoin the outward junction of the Cotswold Way.

10. Turn right at the gate by the quarry here, and follow the track as it speeds downhill virtually all the way into Snowshill. You're unlikely to meet any cars until you reach the first houses, but it is a possibility – as I discovered on the steepest downhill section – so watch out and be prepared to slam on the brakes, and take an equal amount of care with walkers.

> ### *Places To Visit:*
> Snowshill Manor
> (NT – tel: 01386 852410);
> Hailes Abbey (EH – tel: 01242 602398);
> Gloucestershire-Warwickshire Steam
> Railway at Toddington
> (tel: 01242 621405);
> Stanway House (tel: 01386 584469).
>
> ### *Pubs and Cafés:*
> The Snowshill Arms at Snowshill;
> The fruit farm café and shop near
> Hailes Abbey;
> The Mount pub at the top of the
> hill in Stanton.

11 Snowshill and the Bourton Downs

On-Road and Offroad

Area: The north of the Cotswolds – a big tour to the south-east of Snowshill with an optional visit to the Cotswold Farm Park. Start and finish at Snowshill at GR:098337.

OS Maps: Landrangers 150/151/163 – Worcester, the Malverns & surrounding area/Stratford-upon-Avon & surrounding area/Cheltenham & Cirencester area.

Route:
Snowshill (GR:098337)
Upper Slatepits/bridleway (GR:106322)
Hornsleasow Farm (GR:122322)
Bourton Downs/bridleway (GR:132322)
Hinchwick (GR:146301)
B4077 (GR:134283)
Chalk Hill (GR:123260)
Cotswold Farm Park (GR:116267)
Temple Guiting (GR:095281)
Taddington (GR:087312)
Stanway Ash Wood/bridleway (GR:081317)
Stanway (GR:068321)
Lidcombe Hill/bridleway (GR:080329)
Cotswold Way/bridleway (GR:083341)
Snowshill (GR:098337)

Nearest BR Station: Kingham.

Nearest Youth Hostel: Stow-on-the-Wold (tel: 01451 830497).

Approx Length: 19 miles (31km).

Time: Allow 3 hours plus stops.

Rating: Moderate. If you include the final diversion to Stanway, you've got a good climb back to the top of Lidcombe Hill.

A third circuit based on Snowshill can be linked to Rides 9 and 10, as the riding is excellent in these parts virtually wherever you go. It crosses some of the same terrain, as well as visiting the delights of the Bourton Downs, with ultimate distance and direction trimmed to suit your inclinations. This might include a visit to the near-by Cotswold Farm Park to make a full day's outing.

1. From the Snowshill car park ride down through the village with the Manor House on the right and church on your left, following the routes of Rides 9 and 10. Ride on up the hill, but this time follow the road round to the left at the top and out to a T-junction by the side of Oat Hill. Turn right here, and after a short distance turn left onto the first signposted bridleway track by a belt of trees on the left.

2. This track leads eastwards, following the woodland past Upper Slatepits on a surface that is generally good to ride but can become a little squelchy in wet weather. As with all forestry there are rather more tracks than the OS map shows, so resist the temptation to stray off to the right and attempt to follow the bridleway, which turns left and then keeps to the northern fringes of the trees rather than running through the middle of the woodland.

3. Cross straight over at the first lane, joining a signposted bridleway track which runs along the side of a wall with woods on the right, bearing out into more open ground with some interesting jumps and bumps as you cross a nature preservation area, before the route drops down the hillside to the buildings at Hornsleasow Farm. Here the bridleway route is not immediately obvious, but it passes to the left of the rather fancy barn, which is the imposing entrance to the big house of the farm.

4. Turn left to ride east along the road, and where the road bends left to head uphill to the north, turn off onto a signposted bridleway track

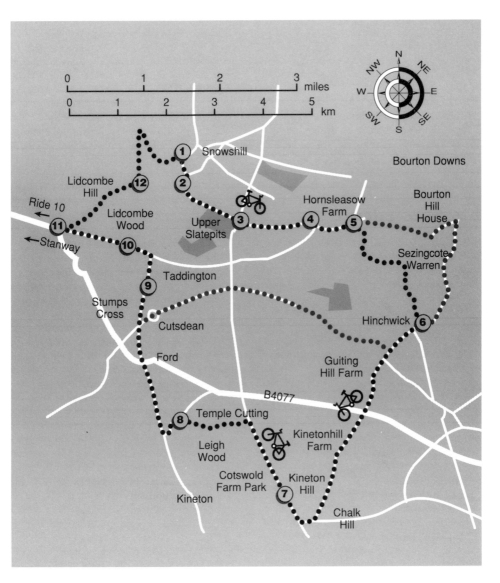

going straight ahead from the apex of the bend.

This follows by the side of a disused quarry, which appears to have become an unofficial rubbish tip, but that is soon left behind as the narrow track – which can be muddy – continues east through the tree line.

5. At the next bridleway signpost a left turn would take you to the top of the Bourton Downs, while the dead-ahead option follows the valley route to the south-east. I opted to follow the valley route, which soon breaks out into the open, crossing several meadows at the foot of the down as it twists east and south into a deep ravine. At one point here I found myself on the wrong side of a fence for no apparent reason, but the signposting is generally good as the valley floor bridleway soon leads to the farmstead at Hinchwick by the side of extensive parkland after more than 1 1/4 miles (2km) offroad. If you ride via the top of the Bourton Downs, you can follow the road south to connect with Hinchwick.

6. From Hinchwick follow the quiet country road as it heads south-east. After less than a mile (about 1km) there's a bridleway turn-off which leads by track and road to Cutsdean, but if it's a nice day you may like to extend the ride to visit the Cotswold Farm Park where they keep a fine stock of rare breed animals. Follow the long lane on across the B4077 for around 3 miles (5km) to Chalk Hill, then take two swift right turns to start heading north with the Cotswold Farm Park coming up after just under a mile (about 1km).

7. From the Cotswold Farm Park continue north along the road. The first left turn comes after just under a mile (about 1km), and then about the same distance further on there's a track on the left that starts by a patch of forest. There is no bridleway signpost, but this is the way, following a good track westwards as far as a barn, and then downhill through woodland to the road at Temple Guiting.

8. Turn left into Temple Guiting, heading downhill through the village and then taking a right turn signposted for Taddington at the next T-junction by the school. Follow this quiet road through very pleasant surroundings for just over 1 3/4 miles (3km), heading straight over the B4077 and into the hamlet of Taddington.

9. From Taddington you can either continue straight on along the road for Snowshill, or extend the route by taking a left turn at the next crossroads on the northern outskirts of the hamlet. This offers an interesting diversion, following a steady uphill to cross the route of

Ride 10 on the edge of Stanway Ash Wood.

10. At Stanway Ash Wood cross straight over the road to join a wide track going into the woodland. Follow the signposted bridleway westwards downhill through Lidcombe Wood with a few lumps and bumps bringing you steeply down to the road to the east of Stanway. If you want a pub at this stage you could latch onto the route of Ride 10 and head for Stanton.

11. To continue the ride you need to head back up the hill. Take the sharp right U-bend by the side of a small farmhouse, and follow the track up Lidcombe Wood. This is a long but steady ascent, and if you have an iron will is ridable most of the way. The woodland is also exceptionally pretty here, so there's nothing to complain about as you head for the top, where you join a hard track leading to an isolated house near the high point of 298m.

12. Follow the hard track as it heads north-east, with the next signpost pointing straight on to join the Cotswold Way bridleway. Turn left to head due north here, following the Cotswold Way for less than a mile (about 1km) along the top of the ridge on the same route as Ride 10, as you open and shut the many gates along the way. You soon come to the quarry, from where it's a sharp right turn through the field gate and a long, fast downhill back into Snowshill.

Places To Visit:
Snowshill Manor
(NT – tel: 01386 852410);
Cotswold Farm Park
(tel: 01451 850307);
Stanway House (tel: 01386 584469).

Pubs and Cafés:
The Snowshill Arms at Snowshill;
The Plough Inn at Ford (just off the route on the B4077);
The Mount at Stanton.

12 South from Bourton-on-the-Water

On-Road and Offroad

Area: The east of the Cotswolds – a tour of the landscape on either side of the River Windrush as it flows south from Bourton-on-the-Water. Start and finish at Bourton-on-the-Water at GR:170206.

OS Maps: Landranger 163 – Cheltenham & Cirencester area.

Route:
Bourton-on-the-Water (GR:170206)
Little Rissington/bridleway
(GR:192197)
Great Rissington/bridleway
(GR:198171)
Great Barrington (GR:207136)
Windrush/bridleway (GR:190132)
Sherborne Common/bridleway
(GR:190153)
Northfield Barn (GR:176153)
New Bridge/bridleway (GR:176177)
Bourton-on-the-Water (GR:170206)

Nearest BR Station: Shipton-under-Wychwood.

Nearest Youth Hostel: Stow-on-the-Wold (tel: 01451 830497).

Approx Length: 17 miles (27km).

Time: Allow 3 hours plus stops.

Rating: Moderate. The bridleway navigation out of Windrush is confusing; otherwise the route is straightforward and fairly easy.

Bourton-on-the-Water is perhaps the ultimate honeypot village of the Cotswolds, a kind of mini Venice, which is pretty but may seem too tripperish and vulgar for some tastes. This vulgarity makes it immensely popular, and in season you are advised to get there early if you wish to leave a car in either of the two main pay-and-display car parks. The circuit that follows explores the countryside to the south and is truly excellent.

1. The first stage takes you eastwards from Bourton to the village of Little Rissington. The most direct way is to follow the fairly minor road, but there is a bridleway alternative for those who are more adventurous. To find this turn left out of the main car park (where the Tourist Information Centre is) by a petrol station. Head out of town towards the A429, which in better times was the Foss Way Roman road, and where the road bends left amidst housing look out for a hard track that bears off to the right and is signposted to the large ponds to the west of Bourton.

At first this is easily followed on a good track, but then I for one lost the way and erred too far south, emerging on the road rather earlier than intended. The correct route continues to the south-east, passing between the lakes to come to the road a little further to the east, but either option is worth exploring.

2. Follow the road as it turns right into Little Rissington, and then on a hard left bend go straight ahead – with care – onto a signposted bridleway track that continues due south to Great Rissington. This is easily followed and offers fast riding. Keep straight on to continue south at the end rather than following the main track which bears off to the east.

3. Where the track hits the road on the outskirts of Great Rissington, keep on south and then bear right on a loop to check out the church and its neighbouring manor house. Follow a slight uphill away from the manor

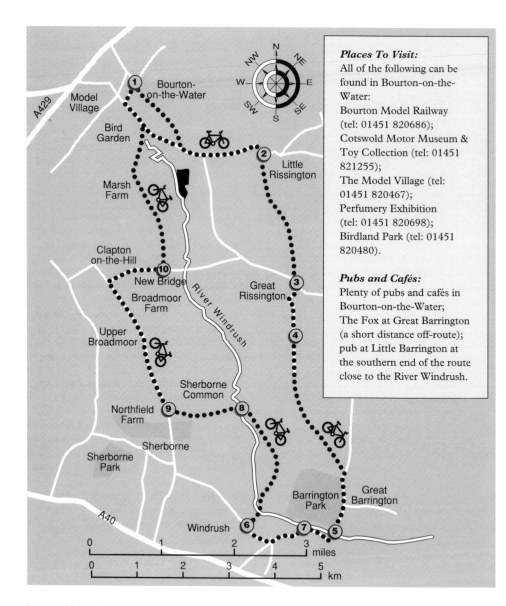

house with a pleasant row of houses on either side, and at the top of the hill look out for a bridleway track that turns right to continue southwards.

4. This section of bridleway starts as tarmac, and then follows a good, hard track along the sides of fields for the next 1 3/4 miles (3km). Ignore the bridleway sign to the right. The way to go is straight on even though there is no bridleway sign, riding up to the next gate with a brilliant, long, curving downhill taking you past

Bourton-on-the-Water represents the Cotswolds as a theme park – it must have been lovely about fifty years ago!

Horseclose Copse and out to a lane a short way north of Great Barrington. This is great riding!

5. Join the road that continues southwards here, skirting the side of the magnificent Barrington Deer Park with a glimpse of a lonely classic temple as you head on down through Great Barrington, keeping right to cross the River Windrush close to a handily placed pub. Turn right here and follow the quiet road westwards, riding on through the hamlet of Windrush, which comes complete with a church and phone box.

6. Just past Windrush Church look for a track turning down to the right by the side of a house. The only sign here says something to the effect of 'No Picnics', but despite the lack of a bridleway sign it is the way to go. After a short distance you come to a couple of houses very pleasantly situated by the river. There are no bridleway signs, which is infuriating when it is not obvious which way to go.

No matter. It is a legal right of way, and in fact the bridleway bears left round the side of the last house to cross a complicated double bend in the River Windrush, after which it bears right across a field beyond a gate with bridleway

signs appearing as you continue northwards on the other side. Keep on across the next field with a belt of trees on the right, and then bear right through the trees as indicated, crossing a bridge and joining a hard track that soon comes up to the most magnificent pile – Manor Farm.

7. The bridleway bears round the right side of Manor Farm, and continues north on a fast, wide track. Not far on, the OS map shows a bridleway option forking left down to the river. In my experience this is not the way to go! You will soon get lost among the long grass and bulrushes with no bridleway to be found, so it's a far better option to keep straight on along the main track for a full ²/₃ mile (1km) past Manor Farm, which brings you to a clearly signposted bridleway and footpath crossroads to the south of Sherborne Common.

8. Here you turn left to cross the River Windrush once again, by means of a sturdy bridge, entering National Trust land with a clear track leading due west across Sherborne Common, and coming out to a lane at Northfield Barn by the fringes of Sherborne Park.

9. Turn right to follow this quiet lane northwards for about 1¹/₂ miles (2.5km), taking the first right turning before Clapton-on-the-Hill. This is the tart of a long, fast downhill – great fun, but don't forget to look out for the bridleway turn-off, which comes after 1,00yd (1km) as the road levels out just before the New Bridge that goes back over the River Windrush as it flows down from Bourton.

10. Turn left onto the bridleway before New Bridge, following it along the side of fields as it heads north, with the possibility of some cowchurned mud as you approach Marsh Farm. From here a quiet residential dead-end lane leads back to the outskirts of Bourton, where such attractions as Birdland Park or the Model Village may or may not delight you.

13 South from Winchcombe

Area: The north-west flank of the Cotswolds above Cheltenham. Start and finish at Winchcombe at GR:026283.

OS Maps: Landranger 163 – Cheltenham & Cirencester area.

Route:
Winchcombe (GR:026283)
Sudeley Lodge/bridleway (GR:040270)
Deadmanbury Gate/bridleway (GR:057262)
Hawling (GR:067230)
Syreford (GR:030202)
Wontley Farm (GR:009247)
Winchcombe (GR:026283)

Nearest BR Station: Cheltenham.

Nearest Youth Hostels: Stow-on-the-Wold (tel: 01451 830497) or Duntisbourne Abbots (tel: 01258 821682).

Approx Length: 15½ miles (25km).

Time: Allow 2–3 hours plus stops.

Rating: Moderate. No real problems here but it's a steady climb out of Winchcombe to start the ride.

This is a brilliant circuit to the south of Winchcombe that takes you on a tour of the high ground above this very pretty Cotswold town. It links with Ride 14 to the north and is accessible from Cheltenham, with some memorable long sections of bridleway and a great downhill.

1. From the centre of Winchcombe ride north-east along the main street, passing the dead-end road that leads via a terrace of alms-houses to the entrance of Sudeley Castle. Take the next very narrow turning on the right, which is Castle Street, following the road for Guiting Power as it crosses the River Isbourne, leaving Winchcombe behind as it starts a steady uphill past the grounds of Sudeley Castle on the right.

2. About 1¼ miles (2km) from the centre of Winchcombe, look for a bridleway sign on the right as the road starts to get seriously steep ahead. Turn off and follow the tarmac drive ahead past some farm buildings, heading south to hug the contours of the hillside past the splendours of Sudeley Lodge, which has a fine view over the castle and town below.

Keep on following the tarmac drive as it climbs steeply round to the left, heading for the top of Round Hill on a gradient that is considerably easier than the nearby road. Ride on to Parks Farm, where the bridleway continues as a rough but easily ridden track. It continues to the hilltop, passing through fields before coming to the road, which crosses from north to south.

3. Cross straight over the road here, joining a narrow bridleway track that goes straight ahead, going east along the side of trees until it meets a lane at Deadmanbury Gate; this is all easy riding. Follow the bridleway sign here, which points 90 degrees to the right, heading south on good tracks for the start of a 2½-mile (4km) long offroad section that has a few gentle ups and downs and is all very agreeable riding. Pass Roel Hill Farm and cross straight over at the next lane, eventually joining a hard track that leads into Hawling.

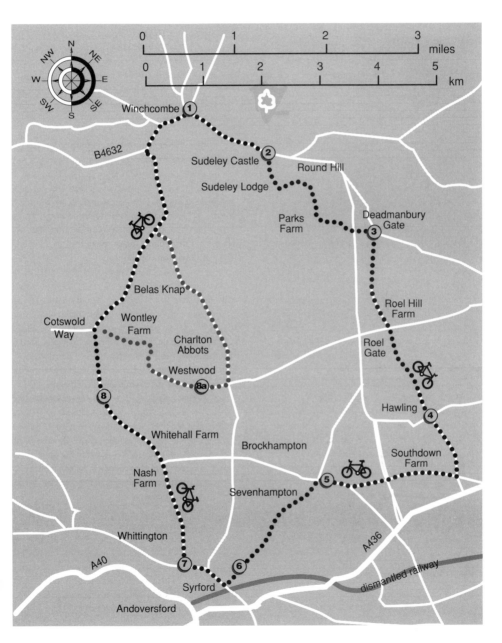

4. At Hawling you come out on the road between a fine house on the corner and a modest chapel. Ride straight on ahead, following the quiet road for less than a mile (about 1km). Then take the first right turn signposted for Winchcombe before you reach the A436, which

The end of the long climb up from Winchcombe –
now you're on the top, you can enjoy the ride with a
great offroad section heading southwards.

can be seen ahead.

Follow this lane westwards over flat country
past Southdown Farm, and continue straight over
the next junction towards Brockhampton, where
there's a possible pub stop in the village.

5. Less than a mile (about 1km) before
Brockhampton a track leads off to the left just
past a trig point; this is a short way beyond the
entrance to Soundborough Farm. Turn down this
track which will speed you south-west on
a very good surface, with 1¼ miles (2km) offroad riding bringing you to the road junction at
Syreford.

6. At Syreford turn right onto the lane that
runs parallel to the A40, which is far enough away
to be muted. Ignore the first right turn into
Brockhampton, and about 500yd (0.5km) further
on take the second right turn, which will take you
to the top of Cleeve Common.

7. The route follows a long, narrow, dead-end
road that meanders northwards for almost 2½
miles (4km). Past the last houses you come to a
small car park for Cleeve Common in surroundings that are very flat and exposed, and to some
extent dominated by the overhead pylons that
march across the landscape.

8. Ride on through the car park, keeping right
to join a rough track that drops downhill to the
ruined buildings of Wontley Farm, hidden in a
small dip. Head up the other side to continue
along a fast track that continues to speed north
toward the ancient long barrow of Belas Knap
(see **8a**). This can be approached on foot by
a footpath and would make a good place
for picnic.

To continue from Belas Knap join the track
that goes straight ahead, passing a farm where you
hit tarmac with a long and very fast downhill all
the way to the outskirts of Winchcombe. The
road crosses the River Isbourne and emerges on
the B4632 by the hospital, from where it's a short
ride back to the centre of town.

8a. It is not totally clear if the 1km section
between Wontley Farm and the footpath leading
to Belas Knap is bike-legal. The alternative is to
turn right at Wontley Farm, following a clear bridleway track that heads eastwards through West
Wood, and then turns left at the next road junction to head north through Charlton Abbots to
reconnect with the route and with the big downhill still ahead of you.

> ***Places To Visit:***
> Information Centre at Winchcombe
> (tel: 01242 602925);
> Sudeley Castle & Gardens
> (NT – tel: 01242 603197).
>
> ***Pubs and Cafés:***
> Plenty of choice in Winchcombe;
> The Craven Arms at Brockhampton.

14 Winchcombe to Bredon Hill

On-Road
and Offroad

Area: The north-west flank of the Cotswolds above Cheltenham. Start and finish at Winchcombe at GR:026283.

OS Map: Landranger 150 – Worcester, the Malverns & surrounding area.

Route:
Winchcombe (GR:026283)
Wychavon Way/Langley Hill Farm/bridleway (GR:010287)
Langley Hill/bridleway (GR:011291)
Gretton (GR:005306)
Alderton/bridleway (GR:000335)
Alderton Hill/bridleway (GR:005345)
Dumbleton (GR:017360)
Wychavon Way/bridleway (GR:002361)
Ashton-under-Hill (GR:997377)
Great Hill/bridleway (GR:985385)
Bredon Hill/bridleway (GR:973395)
Beckford (GR:978358)
Alderton (GR:000335)
Gretton (GR:005306)
Stanley Pontlarge/bridleway (GR:000303)
Stanley Mount/bridleway (GR:002291)
Langley Hill Farm/Wychavon Way (GR:010287)
Winchcombe (GR:026283)

Nearest BR Station: Cheltenham.

Nearest Youth Hostel: Stow-on-the-Wold (tel: 01451 830497).

Approx Length: 23 miles (37km).

Time: Allow 4 hours plus stops.

Rating: Moderate/Hard. There is plenty of hill climbing, you need to take care with navigation on Bredon Hill, and the distance is long enough.

This circuit takes in three hills to the north of Winchcombe – Langley Hill, Alderton and Dumbleton Hill, and Bredon Hill. Bredon Hill is the real challenge and justifies a ride in its own right. To do it justice you are advised to allow plenty of time to enjoy the ups and downs and occasional navigational problems of this route.

1. The long stay car park in Winchcombe is set back to the north-west of the main street. From here turn right onto a dead-end lane signposted as part of the Wychavon Way. This leads out of Winchcombe past the last few houses of an estate, and then heads steeply, steeply uphill with fine views opening out behind. Keep on up to Langley Hill Farm. You may find temporary wire fences across the track designed to steer cows in the correct direction in the farmyard, but these are easily circumvented.

2. Ride straight on through the farmyard leaving the tarmac behind, bearing round to the right by the last barn near the top of Langley Hill, which brings you onto a bridleway that swings due north on a good track to the very top of Langley Hill. It then goes through a gate to join a much rougher track that jolts down the other side, and eventually brings you out to a lane to the west of the hamlet of Greet.

3. Turn left along the road here and follow it to the church at Gretton. Here you take the right turn signposted to Alderton, some 1 3/4 miles (3km) to the north with an uncomplicated crossing of the A438 along the way. Follow the road into Alderton, passing the pub on the right and looking for the signposted bridleway track which goes straight ahead where the road bends left.

4. This bridleway takes you north from Alderton, winding round the right perimeter of a field, and then going uphill to a gate where it enters the woods of Alderton Hill. From here a track heads fairly steeply up through the woodland, eventually bringing you to the top of Alderton Hill, where a bridleway crossroads – the

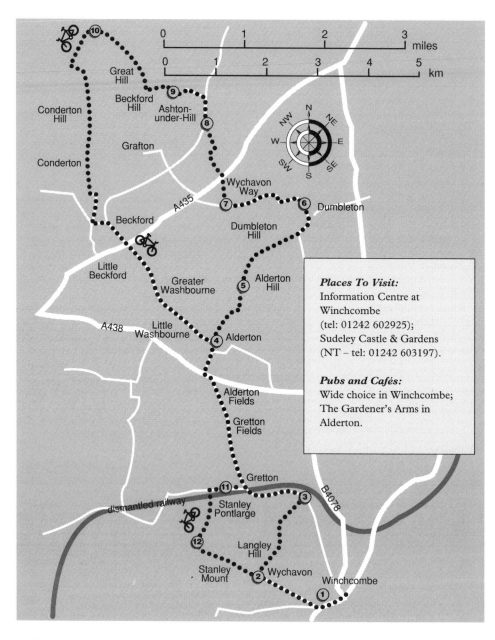

Places To Visit:
Information Centre at
Winchcombe
(tel: 01242 602925);
Sudeley Castle & Gardens
(NT – tel: 01242 603197).

Pubs and Cafés:
Wide choice in Winchcombe;
The Gardener's Arms in
Alderton.

tracks here are shown by red signs – gives the
option of turning left to follow the Wychavon Way
on a direct route, or carrying straight on down the

side of Dumbleton Hill.

5. The Wychavon Way looked fairly muddy

after wet weather, so Dumbleton Hill was the way I chose to go, following a hard, fast track which soon gets a tarmac surface as it hairpins down the hillside, with the solid mass of Dumbleton Hall coming into view. This is a fine old pile that has been turned into a grand hotel, but from the hillside the effect is totally ruined by the packed car park, which is insensitively placed alongside the main building. It's amazing how a collection of shiny tin boxes can mess up the landscape.

6. From Dumbleton follow the road round to the left, heading eastwards towards the A435. After about 1¼ miles (2km) on-road you come to the Wychavon Way bridleway crossing by an isolated house on the corner, which would be a good way to return if you are ready to head back to Winchcombe.

7. To continue for Bredon Hill, turn right at the Wychavon Way/bridleway signpost. A good track leads straight across fields to cut the corner of the A435, which it crosses by overhead power lines. It continues along a much narrower track past orchards, bearing right towards a disused railway bridge and then turning left to join the road on the outskirts of Ashton-under-Hill.

8. Turn right through Ashton-under-Hill, heading north before taking the second dead-end turning on the left – this is before you come to the second church in the village. A narrow lane leads fairly steeply uphill past some prosperous houses, eventually leading up to a solitary house on the hillside with a large and grandiose stable building plus suitable horses to match. From here on the going becomes much harder. You go through a gate onto a rough, tough track that leads up the hillside, and then bears round to the right with the option of a gateway straight ahead. There are no bridleway signposts, and some ingenuity and a good sense of direction is needed to find the way to the summit.

9. Go through the gate that's straight ahead, then bear left along the hillside – this is

Beckford Hill – and from there turn up to the top of the hill, where you should be able to pick up two bridleway arrows that will send you along the top of Great Hill. Time is of the essence on Bredon Hill, and you should allow plenty of it to find the correct way along the bridleway that runs north-west between Great Hill and the radio mast on Bredon Hill, a route of exploration on which I leave you to your own devices.

10. The best way down from this mighty hill is to join the hard, fast track that leads due south for almost 1¾ miles (3km) into Beckford. This is a magical descent that makes up for any hardships on the hill, after which the most direct route back to Winchcombe is a long plug of some 4½ miles (7km) along the flat roads to Greeton via Alderton.

11. Turn right by Greeton Church signposted for Gotherington. About 500yd (0.5km) along the lane here a left turn by an old railway bridge is signposted to Stanley Pontlarge, close to what appears to be an old sentry box in an unlikely setting. Follow the narrow lane under the old railway and uphill to a few houses, bearing right by the side of a modernized house to start the long climb up the hillside, which follows a clear if difficult-to-ride track in a southerly direction.

12. Near the top, this track passes the entrance to a solitary house hidden on top of a hillock, before coming up to a large steel field gate with a mass of helpful bridleway signs. Take the left turn up the side of the field here, heading for the top of Stanley Mount and taking the central track, which keeps to the right of the belt of trees on the hillside. This leads up and over the top, following good tracks by the right side of fields to the east, and soon comes down to the turn-off of the outward route above Langley Hill Farm. From here you can thrill your way back down the steep hill into Winchcombe – and it is steep indeed.

15 The Cotswold Water Park

**On-Road
and Offroad**

Area: The south-east fringes of the
Cotswolds, near to Cirencester – a tour
of the flatlands of the Cotswold Water
Park. Start and finish at Cricklade at
GR:100935; alternatively start from the
B4696 railway arches car park at
GR:064962.

OS Map: OS Maps: Landranger 163 –
Cheltenham & Cirencester area.

Route:
Cricklade (GR:100935)
Cricklade-South Cerney cycle path
(GR:091938)
B4696 car park (GR:064962)
Cycle path bridleway junction
(GR:078949)
Waterhay Bridge (GR:060932)
Ashton Keynes (GR:044940)
Cotswold Community/bridleway
(GR:036953)
South Cerney/cycle path/bridleway
(GR:057970)
Cycle path turn-off (GR:048978)
Driffield (GR:072996)
Manor Farm/bridleway (GR:077989)
Ampney Brook/bridleway (GR:085993)
Down Ampney (GR:098971)
Down Ampney Airfield Memorial/
bridleway (GR:106957)
Cricklade (GR:100935)

Nearest BR Station: Swindon.

Nearest Youth Hostel: Duntisbourne
Abbots (tel: 01285 821682).

Approx Length: 23 miles (37km) full
circuit; 11 miles (17.5km) half circuit.

Time: Allow 2–3 hours plus stops.

Rating: Easy on half circuit. Moderate
on full circuit where mud could be a
problem on the bridleway section after
Driffield.

*This ride explores the flat country between
Cirencester and Cricklade on the flank of the
Cotswold Hills, and in particular the strange
mass of lakes that forms the Cotswold Water
Park. On the west side of the A419 the riding
is very easy and can be recommended for a
family outing; if you extend the ride to the
east of the A419, the distance doubles and
the route becomes a little – but not a lot –
more challenging.*

*You can start this ride from the centre of
Cricklade, which, despite the proximity of
the noisy A419, is a fairly peaceful Cotswold
town that retains some of its old-world
charm; alternatively, there are a number of
handily situated car parks in the midst of the
Cotswold Water Park. The most convenient
of these car parks is on the north side of the
B4696, about a mile (1.5km) south-west
of the A419, and is easily to spot as you
have to drive in through a series of old
railway arches. Note that there is a height
limit here designed to keep out over-
night campervans.*

From Cricklade:

1a. There is a convenient car park in the main
street close by the church. From here ride out on
the B4040 signposted to Leigh and Minety, taking the last right turn on the outskirts of the
town. This should lead you to a recycling centre
and games fields on the western fringes of
Cricklade by Horsey Down, which is where the
railway path/bridleway starts that leads to South
Cerney, about halfway to Cirencester. An alter-

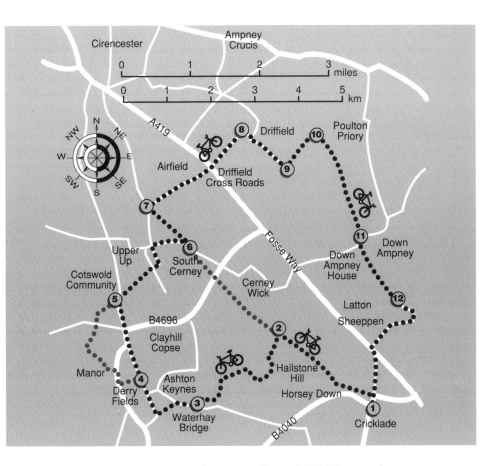

native and possibly more pleasant route is to walk your bike through the churchyard of the big church in Cricklade, and find your way through residential back streets to the games fields and railway path.

It is amazing that there is no signpost for the Cricklade/South Cerney railway path, which starts by the right side of a large municipal building. From there it follows an excellent track that takes you straight out into pleasant countryside, passing through a few gates before crossing a very small version of the River Thames on a substantial bridge. Soon after, it comes to a three-way bridleway sign that points straight ahead to South Cerney and left to Ashton Keynes, which is the route to follow.

From the B4696 car park:

1b. The railway tunnel car park is situated right by the side of the old railway, which is now a cycle path. Turn right under the bridge and cross the B4696 with care as the traffic goes fast here. Follow the track for less than a mile (about 1km) south-east to another tunnel by an old gravel pit, and carry straight on for about 500yd (0.5km) until you reach the three-way bridleway signpost, turning right for Ashton Keynes.

2. The bridleway from the old railway line to Ashton Keynes winds its way through a landscape that is dominated by a handful of the many lakes that form the Cotswold Water Park, all of which were created from old excavations.

Away from the hustle of the A419, you and your bike are in a quiet and remote landscape.

It is well signposted and very easy to follow, but there are warning signs saying that these tracks are prone to flood in very wet weather. Follow the signs towards Ashton Keynes, passing the dire warnings of 'Quicksand', and then turn left by the last lake, where a bridleway signpost points right for South Cerney close to the Waterhay Bridge.

3. Ride out through the car park onto the road here, turning right away from the Waterhay Bridge and following this quiet, country road west for 500yd (0.5km). Where the road bends right, you will see a signposted bridleway turn-off through a gate on the left. Follow this track across fields and over a stream, joining a wide, hard track that brings you to the road on a bend at High Bridge. Turn right here, and follow the road into Ashton Keynes, which is a pretty enough village.

4. From Ashton Keynes the OS map shows a bridleway track turning east off the B4696, and then heading north between two large lakes before it meets the Somerford Keynes Road.

To find this track, turn left by the pub on the corner in Ashford Keynes, and then right along the B4696, which is a quiet road. Just past a footpath and a stream, the bridleway is shown following the driveway to Manor House, which was being rebuilt when I passed by. From here it is easily followed through somewhat bleak surroundings, but unfortunately comes up against a locked gate when you hit the road.

This puts the use of this bridleway in some doubt. The safe option is to continue on-road through Ashton Keynes, turning left for Somerford Keynes and following this road for just over 500yd (0.5km) to the entrance drive to the Cotswold Community, which is directly opposite the end of the track through the lakes. Ride along this drive for a short distance, and then take the first track on the right which follows the side of a field out to the Siddington Road, and is well surfaced with patches of incongruous tarmac.

5. Turn left onto the road, and then after a short distance turn right onto a bridleway track that continues north-east for less than a mile (about 1km) to South Cerney and is pleasant and easy riding. Turn left when you hit the road in South Cerney, and then at the next road junction turn right through the village until you reach the eastern outskirts of the town with the road signposted to Cerney Wick and Down Ampney.

6. Here you have the option of finishing off the ride, by following the road round to the right to join the cycle path. This leads into the railway track/bridleway, heading south-east with less than a mile (about 1km) of easy riding back to the B4696 car park and just over 3¾ miles (6km) to Cricklade.

Alternatively, it makes an interesting ride to extend the route to the east side of the A419. Turn left off the road at the bridleway sign by the bridge on the eastern fringes of South Cerney, and follow the signs that point the way left through the railway arches to join another section of the old railway, this time heading north-west in the direction of Siddington.

The track passes through woodland with an interesting raised section, reaching the road after a modest distance. From here no more of the old railway is open to cyclists, and one wonders why it cannot continue all the way to Cirencester.

7. Turn right for Driffield, crossing the A419 with care. In other respects you can expect quiet, pleasant riding along a narrow country lane.

8. When you enter Driffield, turn right and right again to join a super-narrow, dead-end country lane, which leads to the farm buildings of Manor Farm.

You join a rough track to the left of the big barn here, and follow it on a fairly good surface into woodland, where the track appears to go straight on ahead. This looks very inviting, but it soon comes to a dead end. The bridleway is less inviting and has no signpost as it takes a 90-degree left turn into the woods.

9. The bridleway track follows the middle of a narrow belt of woodland as far as the Ampney Brook. It twists and turns, with a few sections well churned by horses, which could make it a nightmare in wet weather. Look out for plenty of tree stumps to trip your wheels on along the way.

10. When you reach the brook, a new bridge leads over it, joining a good track that soon comes to a crossing track to the south of Ampney St Peter. There are no bridleway signs here, but you turn right, going through a field gate and following a clear track along the side of a field, which soon joins a hard track by a barn. This runs south for more than 1¼ miles (2km) of dead straight riding, passing Poulton Hill Farm with several gates to be negotiated before you reach the outskirts of the village of Down Ampney.

11. Follow the road round to the right in Down Ampney, and then bear left at the green to join the narrow dead-end road that leads to Down Ampney House. This is a very splendid Cotswold mansion set next to the attractive and secluded church by an avenue of trees.

From here you follow the left-hand track ahead through a gate, bearing south-east until you ride out onto the runway of the old Down Ampney airfield.

Ride on along the wide concrete runway, and pause by the memorial that commemorates the men who took off from here at the start of the D-Day invasion. They were carried in gliders towed by Dakotas, and they must have been cold and very frightened at the though of what lay ahead of them. Many were lost and injured as the gliders crash-landed on French soil.

12. Ride straight on from the memorial until a bridleway sign shows you the way onto a track that continues in the same south-easterly direction as the runway bends round to the left. This track soon brings you to a lane, from where a right turn leads back to the A419 about a mile (1.5km) distant. Cross straight over here (with care), using the old road junction straight ahead, which is now closed to cars. From here turn left and ride back into the centre of Cricklade, with a pleasant ride ahead back along the old railway line if you started the ride from the B4696 railway bridge car park.

Places To Visit:
Information Centre at Cirencester (tel: 01285 654180);
Brewery Arts (tel: 01285 657181) at Cirencester;
Corinium Museum (tel: 01285 655611) at Cirencester;
The Butts Farm (tel: 01285 862205) is a working farmstead 3 miles (5km) south-east of Cirencester.

Pubs and Cafés:
Choice of pubs in Cricklade; pub in Ashton Keynes.

16 Bibury and Beyond

On-Road and Offroad

Area: The west flank of the Cotswolds near Cirencester – a tour of the gentle hills around Bibury. Start and finish at Bibury at GR:119067.

OS Map: Landranger 163 – Cheltenham & Cirencester area.

Route:
Bibury (GR:119067)
Bibury Farm bridleway crossroads (GR:123082)
Oldwalls Farm (GR:112098)
Saltway Farm/bridleway (GR:104109)
Ablington/bridleway (GR:101077)
Arlington/bridleway (GR:105065)
Coneygar Wood (GR:127048)
Coneygar Farm/bridleway (GR:132049)
Quenington (GR:143047)
Coln St Aldwyns (GR:145056)
Bridleway (GR:137063)
B4425/bridleway (GR:127077)
Bibury (GR:119067)

Nearest BR Station: None within easy reach.

Nearest Youth Hostel: Duntisbourne Abbots (tel: 01285 821682).

Approx Length: 20 miles (33km).

Time: Allow 3 hours plus stops.

Rating: Moderate. Be prepared for plenty of gentle ups and downs, and possibly severe mud in wet weather.

The area around Bibury offers some excellent offroad biking in easy, rolling terrain with pretty villages along the way. Take note that Bibury is a real chocolate box of a Cotswold village, and is likely to get packed out with car-borne trippers in peak season.

1. If you arrive by car you can park in Bibury on the stretch of road opposite the old cottages of Arlington Row by the side of the river. It's a pleasant spot, but on no account let your car stray onto the double yellow lines, where the local police do much good work.

From here, follow the road south-east through the village towards the church, which is down in a one-way dip and well worth investigating. The road itself swings uphill to the left, passing the loop leading to and from the church. Keep on up the hill for a short distance, and then turn onto the first narrow lane on the left, which has one of those dead-end signs that are such good news for offroad riders.

2. Follow this lane fairly steeply uphill, eventually coming up to a substantial stone house. The bridleway track continues straight ahead to the left of this house (even if it is unsignposted), leading north across fields to the west of Bibury Farm. The worst of the climb is past, but some of the track can be bumpy and muddy with cows wandering about, as the bridleway passes a lonely barn before reaching a clear bridleway crossroads by a gate and a wall.

3. Turn left at the bridleway crossroads, and follow the clear track for just over 1¼ miles (2km) to the north-west until you reach the next road junction. The going along here is variable, with some lumpy and potentially muddy bits along the way, passing through open country on the lonely high ground of this part of the Cotswolds. At the next road junction by Oldwalls Farm go straight ahead on the bend, and follow the quiet road along the Salt Way in the same direction for approximately a mile (1.5km) until you reach Saltway Farm.

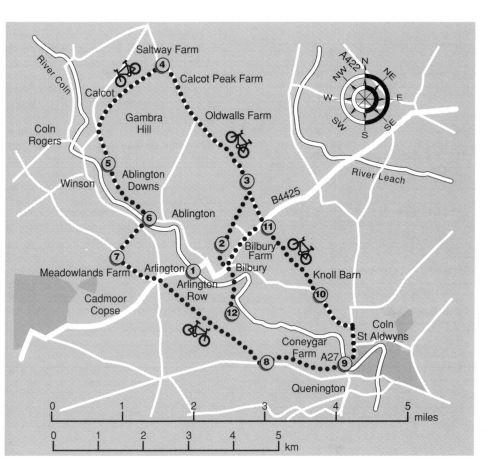

4. A short uphill takes the road past Saltway Farm. Turn left onto a track by the nearside of the farmhouse, and follow this good, fast lane in a south-west direction along the side of Gambra Hill for around 1¼ miles (2km) until you reach the next road junction. Here you immediately swing left onto another bridleway track, heading south-east towards Ablington Down.

5. The track passes an isolated house to the left, and then starts to dip up and downhill, eventually diving down to a very large puddle by the side of woods, which effectively cuts off the track. You can either risk riding through here, or divert around the edge and try to avoid the marshy ground. In wet weather this operation could be a nightmare. Keep on along the track, and follow it on a fast downhill into the hamlet of Ablington, where a very smart terrace of houses lines the bank of the River Coln.

6. You may like to explore the rest of Ablington; otherwise bear right over the river bridge, and follow the road on a short, sharp uphill, crossing straight over the next road to join a steep section of gravelled bridleway that goes straight ahead. This takes you south-west on a good track that heads on for Cadmoor Copse and Barnsley Wood, but that's the wrong way for Bibury and at the next road junction

Take time to check out the bridleway that passes the front of the Ebury Court Hotel in very fine surroundings.

you turn left.

7. Follow the road to the south-east, passing Meadowlands Farm and arriving at a complex crossroads on the outskirts of Arlington. Cross straight over here, and go through a field gate to join a bridleway track that continues south-east and gives you about 3 miles (5km) of offroad riding on the way to Coln St Aldwyns. The track is easily followed and mainly follows a good surface, with the occasional blue bridleway arrow to reassure you that you are on the right route.

8. A steep downhill followed by an equally steep uphill brings you up to the road by Coneygar Wood. Turn left along the road for about 50yd here, turning left off the road just past the side of the last cottage, to follow a signposted bridleway that leads across fields. From there it passes between Coneygar Farm and its outbuildings, going in front of the farm cottage before following a track across a field and down through woodland.

From here a final downhill leads to a bridge across the River Coln on the outskirts of Quenington.

9. Continue the ride by crossing the river bridge and riding up into the hamlet of Coln St Aldwyns, where another pub awaits you at the top of the hill. Keep on north from here, taking the first left turn signposted to Bibury, with gentle ups and downs through peaceful surroundings.

10. After less than a mile (about 1km) the road bends left in a dip. An unsignposted track goes straight ahead here which is bridleway. Follow it on a steady uphill that takes you north-west by the side of fields, until you reach the B4425 close by Bibury Farm, a mile (1.5km) further on.

11. At the B4425 you can turn left for a fast downhill along the road into Bibury, or continue straight ahead on the bridleway for a further stint offroad, turning left at the next bridleway crossroads where you pick up the outward route.

12. Back in Bibury it's worth exploring the church, and also the track that goes south past the front facade of the Ebury Court Hotel which is a magnificent house let down by the rows of shiny cars parked in front of it. The bridleway crosses the River Coln in very fine surroundings here, snaking between some interesting old buildings and then entering open country at the top of a short hill. From here you can follow it down past The Grove, with a short, steep downhill leading to the banks of the River Coln. Past here the bridleway seems to disappear and footpaths take over, although local horseriders appear to make good use of the area.

Places To Visit:
Arlington Mill Museum at Bibury
(tel: 01285 740368);
Bibury Trout Farm (tel: 01285 740215).

Pubs and Cafés:
The Catherine Wheel at Bibury where you can also find a seasonal café;
The New Inn at Coln St Aldwyns.

17 Round 'Little Switzerland'

Area: The mid-Cotswolds, to the north of Cirencester and Stroud – a tour of a wonderful area of small, steep hills and winding roads. Start and finish at Duntisbourne Abbots at GR970079; alternatively start from Bisley at GR:904060.

OS Map: Landranger 163 – Cheltenham & Cirencester area.

Route:
Duntisbourne Abbots (GR:970079)
Middle Duntisbourne/bridleway (GR:983082)
Pinkbury Park/bridleway (GR:963053)
Gloucester Beeches/bridleway crossroads (GR:946049)
Daneway (GR:939033)
Tunley (GR:932045)
Waterlane/bridleway (GR:923047)
Rectory Farm/bridleway (GR:909054)
Bisley (GR:904060)
Battlescombe (GR:920061)
Edgeworth/bridleway (GR:947059)
Knightswood Common (GR:952061)
Duntisbourne Leer (GR:976076)
Duntisbourne Abbots (GR:970079)

Nearest BR Station: Stroud.

Nearest Youth Hostel: Duntisbourne Abbots (tel: 01285 821682).

Approx Length: 16 miles (26km).

Time: Allow 3 hours plus stops.

Rating: Moderate. There are some good climbs here, and you could get muddy problems in wet weather.

The area between the arms of the A419 and A417 to the west of Cirencester offers a real 'little Switzerland' with up and down riding and hidden delights that are quite different from, and tougher than, anything else on offer in the Cotswolds. This ride out of the hamlet of Duntisbourne Abbots gives a good view of this 'secret' part of Britain.

Duntisbourne Abbots makes a good place to start this ride if you are staying at the youth hostel, which can be highly recommended. It's in an old rectory which is pleasantly stuck away, and is both comfortable and practical as youth hostel standards go. In other respects parking in this small village is difficult, and you may do better to start from the larger village of Bisley at the western extremity of the route which also connects with Rides 18 and 19.

1. From Duntisbourne Abbots follow the narrow road for 1¼ miles (2km) south-west through Duntisbourne Leer to Middle Duntisbourne, with a few up and down switchbacks along the way. Just past the turn-off for Middle Duntisbourne, look out for a bridleway on the right, which is clearly signposted.

2. From Middle Duntisbourne follow this track due west across fields. It is easy to follow and good riding with plenty of trees to add interest, but beware of thorns – I got most of many Cotswold punctures along the way here.

3 At the second road junction you come out by a lodge, with a gate into private woodland straight ahead. Turn left to follow the road south for about 500yd (0.5km), and just past the entrance to Pinkbury Park turn right as shown by a bridleway sign which leads you back onto the Pinkbury Park drive.

4. Follow the Pinkbury Park drive past the fine house at the end in a beautiful valley setting, and then continue on down into the valley, following a rough track that bears right at the bottom through woodland to cross a stream.

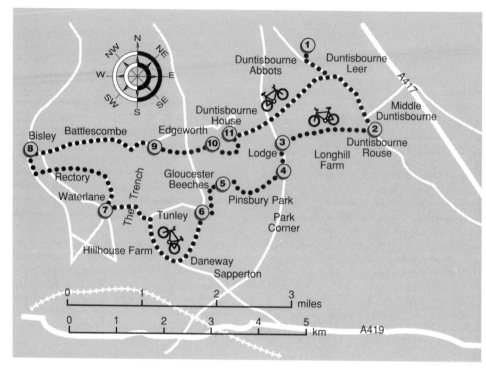

From here it heads up the opposite hillside on a narrow track, which is sometimes unridable and could be very muddy, but makes up for it by passing through some very pretty surroundings. Keep on up the hill, coming up to a field gate by the edge of the woods at Gloucester Beeches, where an old farm building shown on the OS map is now demolished.

5. At Gloucester Beeches the bridleway heads due west across the fields ahead which appear to be preserved for training the local polo ponies – this is smart country! Watch out for the electric wire fences that are extremely unpleasant if touched with a sweaty part of your body. At the poorly signposted bridleway crossroads turn left down a narrow track (signposted as footpath but clearly bridleway), which follows the side of a field. Keep on until you reach the next crossing track, where you turn right for a short pedal to the road.

6. Turn left here, heading south for Daneway, with a long, steep downhill to the bottom of the valley, where you'll find the pub in a fine position by the side of the River Frome. What goes down must go up, and having hopefully refreshed yourself it's a steady uphill on narrow roads signposted to Tunley and Waterlane, weaving and winding round the sides of valleys until you enter the hamlet of Waterlane some 1¼ miles (2km) out of Daneway.

7. Turn right in Waterlane, taking the left forking lane with a dead-end sign, which goes north for Rookwood and then bears left down to a small patch of trees. Here you join a rutted crossing track – plenty of mud here if it's wet – turning left to head due west for the road by Rectory Farm. Cross straight over the road here, and follow the bridleway through to the next road junction, where you turn right along the road into Bisley.

This is real up and down countryside that has more in common with the West Country than most of the Cotswolds.

8. Bisley is a sizeable village with the benefit of a pub, and it makes a good alternative start point to Duntisbourne Abbots. From the church take the dead-end road that goes due east away from the village, signposted for Battlescombe. This starts like a regular country road, but as it winds down into the valley at Battlescombe the road degenerates into a rutted track amid very fine surroundings. Continue steeply up the other side of the valley, zig-zagging up the hillside through a small patch of forestry until you come to a modern forestry barn on the eastern edge of the woodland. Just past here look for a bridleway sign pointing right along the side of a belt of trees.

9. Follow the bridleway along the trees and across open ground, heading eastwards to the next road junction. Here you cross straight over onto the next section of bridleway by the side of a lodge. The bridleway goes down the hill before bearing left up to a gate leading into the quaint hamlet of Edgeworth. Here you ride on to the church by the magnificent manor house, where a bridleway sign points the way up the front drive.

10. In fact the bridleway at Edgeworth Manor turns right off the drive to follow a path through the manor gardens, and very fine and beautiful they are too. It's a rare treat to be able to ride through such surroundings, so don't spoil it but ride with courtesy and consideration. Most owners of such properties would do everything in their power to get such a bridleway diverted, and we owe the owner of this particular manor a vote of thanks. From the gardens the bridleway leads down through some wonderful old iron gates, crossing a stream at the bottom of the valley and then heading fairly steeply up to a quiet lane by Knightswood Common.

11. From here it is a steady plod to the top of the hill on Knightswood Common. Cross straight over at the next crossroads, and follow the road for just over 1¼ miles (2km) back to Duntisbourne Abbots via Duntisbourne Leer, which has a remarkable water splash in a picture-postcard setting – when the sun is shining it really is very pleasant cycling in these parts!

Places To Visit:
Miserden Park Gardens
(tel: 01285 821303);
Painswick Rococco Garden
(tel: 01452 813204);
both off route but within easy reach of the circuit.

Pubs and Cafés:
The Daneway at Daneway;
The Bear at Bisley.

18 The Miserden Trail

*This is a second tour of the steep hills and
thrills that lie between the A419 and A417 to
the west of Cirencester. It is as rewarding
and physically taxing as Ride 17, exploring
marvellous countryside, which makes it
well worth choosing a dry, sunny day when
you can appreciate the surroundings at
their best.*

1. Once again a good start point for the ride is
the Duntisbourne Abbots youth hostel, while
suitable alternatives to start from might include
the villages of Miserden or Sheepscombe. From
Duntisbourne Abbots take the road that heads
west, and on the outskirts of the village bear
right onto a lane, which links to the Winston-
Sapperton road at Jackbarrow Farm.

2. Cross straight over here, joining a bridleway track by the side of Jackbarrow Farm that
heads north-west, and then bear right at the end
of the main track to follow the bridleway north
through the woodland above Ashcombe
Bottom, where it's good riding on an up and
down trail. When you come to a crossing track,
turn left steeply downhill to join the road at
Parson's Hill by the Mitsubishi Offroad Test
Centre. This last section is not shown as
bridleway, but is the only link to the road and is
widely used by local horseriders. Please use it
with discretion.

3. From Parson's Hill follow the road westwards through very up and down countryside.
At the turn-off for Miserden you may like to
stop at the pub in the centre and then explore
the delights of Miserden Park Gardens.

4. From Miserden head back to the turn-off
at Lypiatt, and continue to ride north-west for a
few hundred yards until you come to the first
bridleway turn-off to the left, where there is a
track that soon leads steeply down to
Honeycombe Farm in a wooded valley. From
here it heads up the other side on a dead-end
lane to the few houses that make up The Camp.

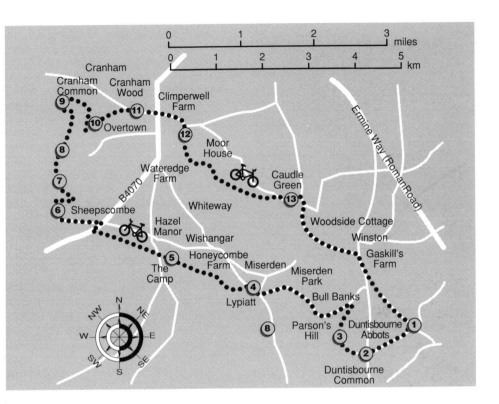

5. Ride straight on at The Camp crossroads, keeping west for another mile (1.5km) to reach the B4070 Stroud road. Turn right here, and then first left, keeping right on a long, fun-filled downhill on the road that takes you deep down into the valley of the village of Sheepscombe, which is a very pretty place indeed.

6. Keep on downhill past the church in Sheepscombe, crossing the river and bearing right to climb up the other side of the valley as far as the pub on the hillside.

Immediately before the pub the route turns right on a lane with a dead-end sign. Follow this on a steady uphill past the backs of houses on the hillside, and then join a rough track signposted as bridleway, which zig-zags up the hillside with fine views opening out over this magnificent valley. Keep on uphill, following the most obvious track past the improbably

sited cricket ground and coming to a bench at a fine viewpoint.

7. From here the bridleway goes into a nature reserve and National Trust woodland, heading north on an up and down track through very fine surroundings. Keep straight on and follow the bridleway as it breaks out into open country on the right side of the woodland, and then as the track drops downhill head straight on at the bridleway crossroads (if you want to cut the ride a little shorter, turn right here).

8. The straight-on option leads downhill on a wonderful woodland track, which gets narrow and difficult to ride in places, eventually reaching the bottom of a valley by an imposing modernized farmhouse with two attendant lakes in a magical setting. Follow the bridleway signs to join the farm track that goes up past the back of

Stop awhile at Miserden and check the map – you may also like to visit the gardens or the pub there.

this building, to head up the opposite side of the valley until you reach the top of the hill by a small cluster of houses at Cranham Common.

9. At the top of the hill you will see an unsignposted track going across the top of the down. Turn along here, or stop for the magical viewpoint, and you soon plunge downhill on another wonderful woodland track that brings you back down the valley.

10. When you arrive at the valley floor the bridleway route becomes a little vague. Go through the gate in the edge of the woodland, turn right through the nearby field gate by a brook, and then bear left up the hill past the exceedingly grandiose homestead at Overtown on the hillside, which looks to be an ideal rich person's retreat. There are no bridleway signs here, but keep on up and then bear left by the side of the Overtown premises until you can turn left onto a track that becomes a driveway leading out to the road by Cranham Wood.

11. Turn right along the road by Cranham Wood, passing the radio masts and crossing straight over the B4070 to continue eastwards

towards Climperwell Farm. At the bottom of the hill look out for the bridleway turn-off to the right, which is clearly signposted along the valley.

12. This bridleway is a very fine track, following the course of a stream southwards through woodland glades. There are a few wiggles and tricky bits as it bears round to the east, passing a boggy section where it turns right and then goes straight on through gates, before joining a hard track that eventually bears uphill away from the valley floor.

As you break out of the woods the most inviting track goes straight ahead, but is not the way to go, or indeed a bridleway. The signposting here is exceedingly vague, but the bridleway appears to turn sharp left uphill by the side of a dense mass of blackthorn, and then turns right along a wall to continue eastwards until it brings you to a gate at the road on the outskirts of Gaudle Green. Here a bridleway sign points back to show that you have indeed been riding in the right direction.

13. Ride steeply downhill through the hamlet of Gaudle Green, and then bear right to head south on a long, steep uphill that eventually leads to a road junction with the Winstone–Sapperton road at Gaskill's Farm. Go straight over here, and join an 'Unsuitable for Motor Vehicles' track that continues south-east, turning into a rough track and giving a lovely offroad section to head back into Duntisbourne Abbots.

Places To Visit:
Miserden Park Gardens
(tel: 01285 821303);
Painswick Rococco Garden is
approximately ⅔ mile (about 1km) from
Sheepscombe (tel: 01452 813204).

Pubs and Cafés:
The Butcher's Arms at Sheepscombe;
pub at Miserden.

19 Cirencester Circuit

**On-Road
and Offroad**

Area: The mid-Cotswolds – a tour to the north of Cirencester. Start and finish at Cirencester Abbey at GR:023020; alternatively, start from Duntisbourne Abbots at GR:970079.

OS Maps: Landranger 163 – Cheltenham & Cirencester area.

Route:
Cirencester Abbey (GR:023020)
A417/Bowling Green Lane (GR:021026)
Baunton/A435 (GR:022043)
A417/Stratton (GR:012038)
Cirencester Park/bridleway
(GR:995028)
Lower End/bridleway (GR:996047)
Daglingworth (GR:993051)
Grove Hill/bridleway (GR:992054)
Duntisbourne Rouse/bridleway
(GR:987060)
Duntisbourne Abbots (GR:970079)
A417/bridleway (GR:991072)
Woodmancote (GR:003088)
North Cerney/bridleway (GR:021079)
Baunton/bridleway (GR:026044)
Cirencester Abbey (GR:023020)

Nearest BR Station:
Kemble, south of Cirencester.

Approx Length: 15 1/2 miles (25km) from Cirencester; 19 miles (31km) from Duntisbourne Abbots.

Time: Allow 3 hours plus stops.

Rating: Moderate. There are no real hills to contend with, but some of the bridleway between North Cerney and Cirencester may seem slightly demanding.

This ride connects the fine market town of Cirencester with the Duntisbourne hamlets. It can be grouped with Rides 17 and 18 which explore the fabulous countryside to the south-west and north-west of Duntisbourne Abbots. Cirencester is a fine town with a magnificent abbey, and makes a good place to start the ride, although you may prefer to start from Duntisbourne Abbots or any other village en route.

Cirencester Park sprawls westwards from the centre of Cirencester, and from an OS map looks as though it should be able to provide an important network of safe cycle routes from the centre of Cirencester into the nearby countryside, but while it is open to walkers and horseriders it is banned to cyclists. All one can do is gaze through the magnificent cast iron ornamental gates, and ask why someone who is fortunate enough to own such a vast tract of land should deem it proper to exclude cyclists and force them to take their life in their hands as they cross the A417 trunk road, which tends to have nose-to-tail traffic on the outskirts of Cirencester.

1. To get to the A417 junction, which will take you out of Cirencester, head north from the Abbey, following the one-way system and then keeping north by turning left through a modern housing estate close to the town's outskirts.

A right turn at the next dead-end road should bring you to a line of bollards next to a phone box by the side of the A417, where great care and a certain amount of nerve is needed to get across to the relative calm of Bowling Green Lane, which is the all-important road to look for.

2. Ride on along Bowling Green Lane, which is a dead-end road that eventually leads to bridleway track at a gate. From here the bridleway heads north along the east bank of the River Churn all the way to North Cerney, a distance of some 3 3/4 miles (6km) that can be fully enjoyed on the return journey. On the way out follow this track for some 1 1/4 miles (2km), crossing the side

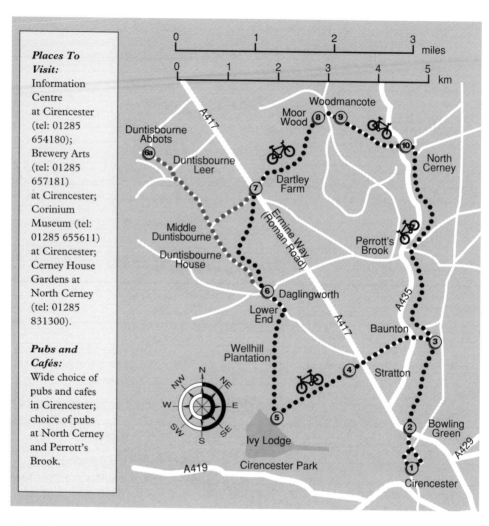

Places To Visit:
Information Centre at Cirencester (tel: 01285 654180); Brewery Arts (tel: 01285 657181) at Cirencester; Corinium Museum (tel: 01285 655611) at Cirencester; Cerney House Gardens at North Cerney (tel: 01285 831300).

Pubs and Cafés:
Wide choice of pubs and cafes in Cirencester; choice of pubs at North Cerney and Perrott's Brook.

of a meadow and then bumping across an open field in conditions that could be gruesome in wet weather but are simply bouncy when dry.

3. At the first road junction you reach the hamlet of Baunton, where you turn left down the road, crossing the River Churn and continuing across the A435. From the A435 follow the road straight on through the outskirts of Stratton, which brings you to the A417. Cross straight over here, joining a dead-end road that bears round to

the right with a clearly signposted bridleway track leading on from a farmyard.

4. From here a very good track leads south-west along the side of fields, with almost 1¼ miles (2km) of offroad riding and an easy uphill leading you to the edge of Cirencester Park near Ivy Lodge, where there's yet another sign announcing that while walkers and horseriders are welcome, cyclists are not.

5. From the Cirencester Park junction a hard track runs due north. Turn sharp right onto this track, passing a beautifully kept polo ground before joining a rougher, tougher track that continues through the Wellhill Plantation to the hamlet of Lower End.

Look for the bridleway sign pointing left here just before you reach the road. It takes you along a pleasant, narrow track by the side of a field, bringing you to the church and the road at Daglingworth, about 500yd (0.5km) to the north.

6. Turn left through Daglingworth, and follow the road north-west signposted for the Duntisbournes. A short way out of Daglingworth a turn-off to the right leads to a pleasant offroad diversion.

Following the dead-end road up Grove Hill, the bridleway starts at a track by the side of the first house on the left. From here the bridleway follows the contours of the hill along the side of woodland, and eventually drops down to the hamlet of Duntisbourne Rouse. From here a clearly signposted bridleway turns off to the right to take you up a narrow track and over the hill to the A417.

To Duntisbourne Abbots and back:
6a. To link in Duntisbourne Abbots, use the road that links the Duntisbourne hamlets. This offers very pleasant cycling, and it's well worth a slight diversion to explore the lower village of Duntisbourne Leer with its impressive watersplash. On the return leg you can ride down through Middle Duntisbourne with its rather shallower watersplash, heading up the other side of the valley to get to the A417 on a quiet road route.

7. Cross the A417 with care. At the time of writing the highway authorities were changing this road into a dual carriageway, which may make this process more difficult. One cannot imagine them bothering to build an underpass for cyclists, walkers and horseriders, which in my view should be mandatory at all crossings of this kind!

In its single-lane state, you turn left along the A417 for about 50yd, and then turn right onto a dead-end lane, which is bridleway leading to Dartley Farm. Ignore the track that goes straight ahead through some trees, and bear right downhill past the farm buildings, joining a pleasant if rough track that goes down and up through the next valley, with the foul odours and noise of the A417 soon left far behind.

8. Climb uphill past Moor Wood, where the track leads out to a lane sandwiched by two very splendid Cotswold houses, which would be suitable for anyone winning the lottery. Ride on up the lane, passing between two entrance pillars to join the road on the outskirts of Woodmancote.

9. Turn right onto the road, and immediately fork left to head south-east to North Cerney; the road signs were pointing in completely the wrong direction when I last rode this way. Enjoy the long, fast downhill to the A435, and then follow the North Cerney signs, riding along the A435 for a hundred or so yards before bearing left into North Cerney, where a bridge takes you across the River Churn by the side of a convenient pub.

10. Ride on up the hillside away from the A435 here, and as the hill steepens look for a bridleway sign on the right. From here the bridleway leads all the way to Bowling Green Lane on the outskirts of Cirencester, with only a short distance on quiet lanes and the rest on tracks where the going is variable and in some places could be awful after wet weather.

The first section sticks quite closely to the River Churn and is not that easy to follow, with the added possibility of cow-churned mud to grind through. Keep high on the hillside to avoid this, only dropping down when you find a clear track. From there on it's a slow but mainly pleasant ride, with some good tracks mixed with a few less bike-friendly sections. There's an opportunity to stop at the pub at Perrott's Brook, and then as the spire of the Abbey comes into view you can make the final thrust for Cirencester.

20 Chedworth and Withington Woods tour

On-Road and Offroad

Area: The mid-Cotswolds to the south-east of Cheltenham – an easy tour of the countryside bordered by the A435, A40 and A429. Start and finish at Andoversford at GR:025198.

OS Map: Landranger 163 – Cheltenham & Cirencester area.

Route:
Andoversford (GR:025198)
A436/bridleway (GR:025183)
Thorndale farm/bridleway (GR:018170)
Withington (GR:032155)
Cassey–Compton/bridleway (GR:049151)
Hilltop road/bridleway (GR:058160)
Yanworth (GR:077138)
Stowell Park (GR:083133)
Pancakehill/bridleway (GR:067112)
Chedworth/bridleway (GR:057122)
Airfield/road junction (GR:042125)
Withington woods/bridleway (GR:036133)
Shill Hill/bridleway (GR:014160)
Thorndale farm/bridleway (GR:018170)
A436/bridleway (GR:025183)
Andoversford (GR:025198)

Nearest BR Station: Cheltenham.

Approx Length: 19 miles (31km).

Time: Allow 3 hours plus stops.

Rating: Moderate. Nothing too challenging on this ride, but mud could make things difficult.

The village of Andoversford, at the junction of the A40 and A436, makes a good place to start this ride, which completes a full tour of the Chedworth and Withington Woods area to the south-east of Cheltenham, visiting some out-of-the-way hamlets by bridleways and lanes.

1. If you arrive by car, you can park in the back street of Andoversford near the handy village store, which appears to sell anything and everything. To start the ride, turn right down the main street of Andoversford (A436) to head westwards for a short distance, and after about 300yd turn left to pass through an imposing set of gates and head due south along a smart tarmac farm drive, which is a bridleway. Continue for approximately 2/3 mile (about 1km) in the same direction, passing through a gate before reaching the southern fork of the A436.

2. The A436 is easy enough to cross here, and a signposted bridleway leads straight on ahead, continuing due south by the side of the golf club. On its way it crosses a stream and a rutted field, before coming up to a lane by a farmstead where you'll more than likely be met by a rather fine flock of goats by the Withington road.

3. Cross straight over the Withington road, joining the driveway that leads up to Thorndale Farm and is signposted as bridleway. Watch out for the rain gulleys cut into the drive – they are truly awful for a bike to hit at any speed except the very slowest.

4. From Thorndale Farm follow the bridleway signs through a gate, and take the left hand direction along the bottom edge of a big, hillside meadow. This takes you south to Upcote Farm, where beyond the peacocks you'll find plenty of sheep and good bridleway signposting. The route leads onto a narrow track heading south-east, and then down into the hamlet of Withington.

5. From Withington head east on the

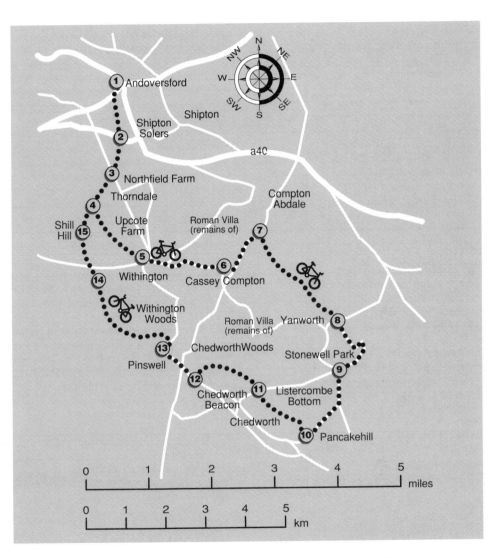

Compton Abdale road, crossing the River Coln and forking right on the lower road that leads to Cassey Compton, where you'll find a most unusual arts centre in an imposing Cotswold building in the valley. About 300yd before you get there, look out for the bridleway turn-off to the left. This is by a barn, on the apex of the right-hand bend just past the overhead power lines.

6. The bridleway from Cassey Compton provides a short cut due east, which leads through to another branch of the Compton Abdale road. Turn left here, with a long, steady uphill ahead of you – at least it's a very quiet road. At the top of the hill start to look out for a clearly signposted bridleway track on the right as the road begins to head downhill to Compton Abdale in the valley.

7. The bridleway along the top here is a great offroad ride of almost $1^3/_4$ miles (3km) as you head south-east for Yanworth. It follows a very good surfaces across high, open country, with a final long, steady downhill into the hamlet of Yanworth. Ignore the left-turning track at about the halfway point, and just keep on ahead all the way.

8. Cross straight over the road at Yanworth to head south downhill for about $2/_3$ mile (about 1km). The road then loops to the left on a sharp uphill, with the first right turn leading you south by the side of Stowell Park. Keep following the road as it bears round to the west to recross the River Coln.

9. At the next crossroads you can divert off-route to investigate the Roman Villa hidden away in Chedworth Woods which has a museum and National Trust shop.

To continue from the crossroads, take the lane going south (left turn from Stowell Park) signposted for Fossebridge. Turn off uphill to the right after Raybrook Farm, with a final downhill zoom into the rambling village of Pancakehill ending an on-road section that is about as pleasant as they come.

10. As you ride into Pancakehill take the first right turn signposted as a dead-end lane. Keep right past a few houses, and you will find your way to the bridleway track, which heads north-west along the hillside, passing some well-tended paddocks along the way. It eventually leads out to the road above Chedworth, where the option of a left-hand turn will take you downhill to the pub.

11. To continue, ride straight across at this road, and follow the clearly signposted bridle-way track, which starts to become a little confusing when it reaches the old airfield on the fringes of Chedworth Woods. The bridleway here has been re-routed. As you join the old concrete runway you follow it round to the south, and keep bearing left along it until you reach the next road junction, which is by the side of a small patch of trees.

12. At the end of the runway turn right along the road, heading north-west to cross the next junction in the direction for Withington.

13. After just over $2/_3$ mile (about 1km) the road heads into Withington Woods. At this point a bridleway track turns off to the left, and is easily spotted by the side of a tall radio mast. The bridleway is fairly easy to follow, as the track heads along the fringes of the woodland, crosses open ground and then bears north beneath the overhead power lines, where you reach a road after almost $2^1/_2$ miles (4km) of very pleasant offroad riding.

14. Cross straight over this road for a short offroad section to the road junction beyond. Here you turn left along the road for 100yd or so, before the next bridleway turn-off to the right takes you along a rough track and into the woodland of Shill Hill. From here it's virtually all downhill along the edge of the woods. There are nice views over the countryside to the east, but while the going is OK in dry weather, it could be pretty grim in the wet.

15. Emerging from the woodland of Shill Hill, the bridleway signs direct you diagonally downhill across a meadow and back to Thorndale Farm. Here you join the outward route, which is the best way to head back into Andoversford.

Places To Visit:
Chedworth Roman Villa
(NT – tel: 01242 890256).

Top Pubs
The Mill at Withington;
The Seven Tuns at Chedworth.

21 Shipton and Salperton circuit

**On-Road
and Offroad**

Area: The mid-Cotswolds – a tour of some fine country to the east of Cheltenham bordered by the A40, A436 and A429. Start and finish at Shipton at GR:037185; alternatively start from Andoversford at GR:025198.

OS Map: Landranger 163 – Cheltenham & Cirencester.

Route:
Andoversford/optional start (GR:025198)
Shipton (GR:037185)
Shipton/bridleway (GR:039187)
Pen Hill (GR:069195)
Salperton Park/bridleway (GR:076197)
Hazleton (GR:080180)
Turkdean/bridleway (GR:107177)
Cold Aston (GR:127198)
Notgrove (GR:110200)
Farhill Farm (GR:091197)
Salperton (GR:076202)
Hampen (GR:058199)
Shipton/bridleway (GR:039187)
Shipton (GR:037185)

Nearest BR Station: Cheltenham.

Nearest Youth Hostels: Duntisbourne Abbots (tel: 01285 821682) or Stow-on-the-Wold (tel: 01451 830497).

Approx Length: 16 miles (26km).

Time: Allow 2–3 hours plus stops.

Rating: Moderate. Nothing too strenuous or difficult here, but there are a few modest hills to be climbed.

This is a ride that has some surprises in store since it boasts some very fine tracks. It can be linked with Ride 20 from Andoversford via Shipton Solers, or you can start from the village of Shipton, which has limited room for roadside parking.

1. From the church in Shipton ride east through the village, taking the first fork to the left. In little more than 50yd you reach the next road junction, where you go straight ahead onto a dead-end lane to join a bridleway that bears east past the last buildings. From here it follows the side of fields on a good track, bringing you to a narrow lane after just over 2/3 mile (about 1km) offroad.

2. Turn right for a steady uphill on this lane, reaching the next road junction at Pen Hill after some 1¼ miles (2km).

3. Turn right onto the road at Pen Hill, and almost immediately left to pass through the imposing entrance gates to Salperton Park. Follow the lane ahead on a steady downhill towards this massive country house on the hillside.

4. You soon come down to a crossroads, which is signposted left to Salperton with a pri-

Shipton and Salperton circuit

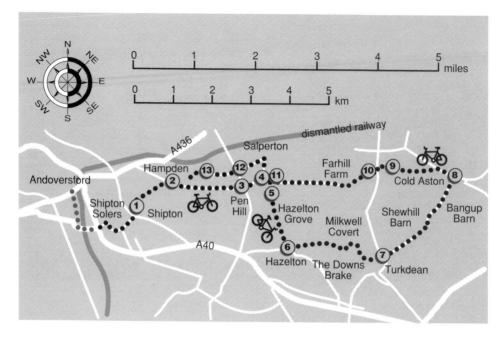

vate road going ahead to the big house. Instead take the dead-end option by turning right here, and follow the lane as it bends round to the east, until you reach a signposted bridleway track turning-off to the right. It's at the top of the hill just past a belt of trees.

5. Follow this bridleway which plunges downhill on a fairly good track, heading south along the side of Hazleton Grove. It then joins a farm drive as it reaches the outskirts of Hazleton after about a mile (1.5km) offroad. Keep on south through Hazleton past the church, and then bear left onto a road marked as unsuitable for vehicles.

6. This road, which goes due east from Hazleton and becomes bridleway, gives a fine ride for 1³/₄ miles (3km) to Turkdean. Passing a farm, the tarmac disappears as the hard track winds its way along a fine valley floor with high hills either side. At the end of the valley a fairly steep uphill leads through a farmyard and onto the road at Turkdean.

7. Turn right onto the road at Turkdean, and then almost immediately left, following a bridleway track down past the side of old buildings for another 1³/₄ miles (3km) of excellent offroad riding. This takes you north-east to Cold Aston, dropping down into a valley to cross a stream; a final steep climb leads past Bangup Barn and from there a ride past the school on a level track leads you into Cold Aston.

8. If you want the pub in Cold Aston turn right. To continue the ride turn left, and after about 500yd (0.5km) you will come to a bridleway that turns off to the left to go due west, following a fine line of beech trees across the fields. It's a somewhat strange track, weaving its way through the trees until it comes to a smart crossing track, where a right and a left turn take you downhill across a meadow.

Go straight up the other side to find a gate which lets you into the smart hamlet of Notgrove, a place where the Manor appears to have a monopoly on access to the church.

Shipton and Salperton circuit

The view from the top. The ride across the Cheltenham hills (Ride 22) gives superb views over the metropolitan sprawl below, before heading off to discover a fine network of tracks and minor roads.

9. Ride through Notgrove and find your way westwards to the main road. Turn left for Turkdean, and then after about 100yd turn right onto a bridleway opposite the ornamental entrance to Notgrove Manor.

10. The farm track leads downhill into the valley, where you come to a clear set of bridleway signs pointing right and straight on. Turn right through the gate here to head up the valley, and then follow the signs through another gate on the left to join a track that plods on a steady but long uphill through the middle of a field – this could be very heavy going in wet weather. Eventually it brings you up to a farm cottage at Farhill Farm, joining a rough tarmac lane that continues west across the top of the land to Salperton Park.

11. Ride on to the Salperton Park crossroads of the outward journey. Take the signposted direction for Salperton, and at the next junction by an enormous crucifix turn left for a steady uphill to the main road.

12. Cross straight over onto the bridleway track that goes ahead, and follow this westwards to the hamlet of Hampen, which is well hidden on the hillside.

13. From Hampen a narrow, almost private, road snakes south uphill, joining the outward route once again for a final fast and furious bridleway descent back to Shipton.

Places To Visit:
Off route at Northleach:
Information Centre at the Cotswold Countryside Collection
(tel: 01451860715);
Keith Harding's World of Mechanical Music (tel: 01451 860181);
one of the finest Cotswold wool churches famous for its collection of brasses.

Pubs and Cafés:
The Plough at Cold Aston.

22 Cheltenham Hills

**On-Road
and Offroad**

Area: The mid-Cotswolds – a fine tour of the high hills to the south of Cheltenham. Start and finish at the Daisy Bank Road car park off the B4070 south of Leckhampton at GR:950188.

OS Maps: Landranger 163 – Cheltenham & Cirencester area.

Route:
Daisy Bank Road car park (GR:950188)
Hartley Hill/bridleway (GR:957184)
Leckhampton Hill/Cotswold Way/
bridleway (GR:951178)
A436/South Hill (GR:946165)
Cuckoopen Barn Farm/bridleway
(GR:946157)
Hill Barn (GR:952147)
Cowley (GR:964147)
Cockleford (GR:969142)
High Cross (GR:968132)
Colesbourne/A435/bridleway
(GR:000133)
Colesbourne Park/bridleway
(GR:998139)
Upper Coberley (GR:981160)
Seven Springs/A436/A435/Cotswold
Way (GR:968171)
Daisy Bank Road car park (GR:950188)
Hartley Hill/bridleway (GR:957184)
Leckhampton Hill/Cotswold Way/
bridleway (GR:951178)
Hartley Hill/bridleway (GR:957184)
Daisy Bank Road car park (GR:950188)

Nearest BR Stations: Cheltenham.

Nearest Youth Hostel: Duntisbourne Abbots (tel: 01285 821682).

Approx Length: 17 miles (28km).

Time: Allow 3 hours plus stops.

Rating: Moderate. Be prepared for some steep hill climbing and watch the navigation.

This is a wonderful ride to the immediate south of Cheltenham. The route is criss-crossed by A roads but they don't interfere, and instead there's a high proportion of top class offroading coupled with some fantastic views and the chance for a very technical final descent.

1. The B40670 heads south from the Cheltenham suburb of Leckhampton. As the mass of houses disappear you come to Daisy Bank Road on the east side of the B4070, which has a handy small car park a short way along. This makes a good place to start the ride.

From the car park follow Daisy Bank Road to the east, steadily gaining height and passing occasional houses along the way. As the houses thin out the bridleway is signposted, bearing off to the right along Charlton Kings Common, and from here it steadily gains height on the contours.

2. The first change in direction comes when a sharp right-turn bridleway sign points the way up a steep, rough track, which I would challenge anyone to ride all the way to the top. It's a hard push, but when you get there everything is worth while, as the views are magnificent.

3. The bridleway signposting is pretty good as you follow the track west along the top of Hartley Hill towards Leckhampton Hill with great views over the seething, sprawling mass of Cheltenham. You will more than likely encounter a few walkers and horse-riders up here, so take care to be considerate, and keep on ahead until you reach a bridleway sign pointing

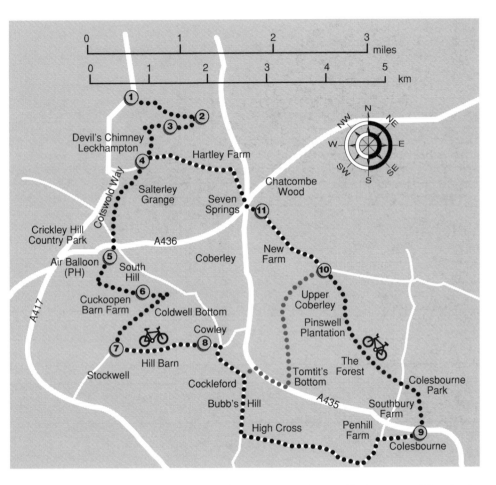

left through a gate. This direction takes you south away from the edge, heading along a track that leads to the road.

(Before you make this turn-off you might like to walk further round the edge – it's footpath not bridleway – to look at the stone stack known as the Devil's Chimney. Those interested in prehistory should note that Leckhampton Hill is also the site of a large Iron Age hill fort.)

4. Turn right at the road and then left after about 100yd, following the Cotswold Way sign as the bridleway track bumps along on a fast downhill with around ²/₃ mile (1km) of offroad

riding before you hit the next road junction by the college.

5. Turn left to ride up to the A436 here, crossing over and joining an unsignposted track that goes straight ahead up South Hill close to a notice for the Woodland Trust. This track climbs steadily towards the top, passing through a gate and then reaching a road, where you turn left to head east along the top on a bridleway track leading on past Cuckoopen Barn Farm, which is surrounded by trees in a bleak landscape.

6. Keep on from Cuckoopen Barn Farm, and

follow the track through fields and then down-hill to the next signposted bridleway junction. Here you turn sharp right through a field gate above Coldwell Bottom, following the hillside on a lovely track. This eventually brings you to the bottom, where a little navigational care is needed to stay on course as there are no bridle-way signs to help you. Ahead you will see a wide tractor track going straight up the middle of a big hill. This is the way to go, keeping south-west to the hilltop where you join the road well to east of the massive radio masts on the top of Shab Hill.

7. Turn left along the quiet road at the top, and follow it eastwards and downhill into Cowley, where the big manor house is home to the Girl Guides. (On the way down the hill there's an alternative bridleway route into the village, but you'll probably go so fast you miss it.)

8. From Cowley the route heads to Coles-bourne, but not by the direct A435. Instead it's much more pleasant to follow quiet lanes along the south side of the valley, heading for Cockleford, where you can make a pub stop, and then climbing up Bubb's Hill. Turn left at the crossroads at High Cross on the hill top, heading along the top for just over 1¼ miles (2km). A left turn underneath the overhead power lines brings you speedily back down the valley, with a right turn taking you directly to the A435 opposite the pub at Colesbourne.

9. Cross the A435 with care, turn right for a short distance, and then turn left off the road by the far side of the pub. This takes you onto an excellent section of bridleway, which starts by heading north along the edge of Colesbourne Park, where you'll see some fine 'distressed' old gates. The bridleway then turns left into the trees to bear north-west on a great track that speeds through The Forest, passing a very iso-lated house along the way and then coming to a strange, semi-round flint cottage on the edge of the Pinswell Plantation. From here the route

crosses open ground before joining the road above Upper Coberley.

10. Go straight ahead on the road above Upper Coberley. Keep straight on as the road bears left, joining a bridleway track that heads down to the A436/A435 junction close by overhead powerlines at Seven Springs.

11. Cross straight over at Seven Springs, and ride about 100yd north on the A435 before bearing left onto a lane signposted as the Cotswold Way. This leads steadily uphill to a left hand bend where the Cotswold Way contin-ues straight ahead as footpath. The lane bears westwards as it continues to climb, and once on top of the down it heads past Hartley Farm to rejoin the outward route by the next Cotswold Way sign.

12. From here the favourite way to return to base is to retrace your wheeltracks to the top of Hartley Hill, where that steep and very rough uphill section is almost as demanding on the way down as it was on the climb. All that remains is a fast ride along Daisy Bank Road to finish off the ride, but remember that this is a residential area and you may meet uncompro-mising cars on the blind corners.

Places To Visit:
Information Centre at Cheltenham (tel: 01242522878);
Cheltenham Art Gallery & Museum (tel: 01242 237431);
The Holst Birthplace Museum (tel: 01242 524846) at Cheltenham;
The Pittville Pump Room Museum (tel: 01242 523852) at Cheltenham.

Pubs and Cafés:
A huge choice in Cheltenham;
pub at Cockleford;
The Colesbourne Inn at Colesbourne.

23 Tetbury Trail

**On-Road
and Offroad**

Area: The mid-Cotswolds – a tour round Tetbury including a short section of the old Foss Way. Start and finish at Tetbury at GR:889933.

OS Map: Landranger 162 – Gloucester & Forest of Dean area; Landranger 163 – Cheltenham & Cirencester area.

Route:
Tetbury (GR:889933)
Chavenage House (GR:873952)
Chavenage Green/bridleway (GR:865957)
Ledgemore Bottom/bridleway (GR:854965)
Barton End (GR:848979)
Avening (GR:880981)
Avening Court/bridleway (GR:893982)
Cherington/Culkerton/Rodmarton junction (GR:915976)
Rodmarton/bridleway (GR:941978)
Culkerton (GR:932959)
Foss Way/byway (GR:947952)
Long Newnton/bridleway (GR:909924)
Tetbury (GR:889933)

Nearest BR Station: Kemble.

Nearest Youth Hostel: Duntisbourne Abbots (tel: 01285 821682).

Approx Length: 20 miles (32km).

Time: Allow 3 hours plus stops.

Rating: Moderate/Easy. Good tracks and the absence of real hills make this an easy ride in dry weather, although the four-wheel-drive-ravaged state of some of the Foss Way is a little trying.

Tetbury is a very pleasant small Cotswold town to start this ride from with a choice of car parks, but likely to get crowded with shoppers. Take time to check out the magnificent church of St Mary if you're into ecclesiastical architecture, and enjoy this excellent ride.

1. From the centre of Tetbury follow the signs for the A433 for Cirencester, and then turn off on the B4014 Avening road. After about 200yd fork left onto a minor road signposted to Chavenage House. This leads you north-west through peaceful countryside, passing the entrance gates to Chavenage House about 1¼ miles (2km) out of Tetbury. It is both homely and magnificent in a small sort of way, and if you are lucky enough to pass by during opening times a member of the family is likely to be the person showing you round.

2. From Chavenage House continue along the road, passing two signposted bridleways on the left. Follow the road as it bends round to the left, and then fork right onto a track – no signpost here but it is bridleway – leading to a solitary house by an avenue of trees at Chavenage Green.

The track passes close to the right side of the house, and then crosses fields on a good surface as it bears north-west. It passes through a gate under the overhead power lines, and then meets a wide gravel crossing track at the next gate close to the overhead power lines at Ledgemore Bottom.

3. Turn right at Ledgemore Bottom, and follow the wide gravel track uphill to the next gate, where it goes into a field. A short way on, the main track bears round to the right, but this is not the way to go. The bridleway, which is well hidden and has no signpost, continues in much the same direction you have been riding, following a hedge at the side of the field on a lumpy, bumpy surface. It then bears left onto a better track between high hedges, which will eventually bring you out to the farm at Barton End.

4. At Barton End a 'Public Path' sign points straight ahead and will cut off the corner, but with

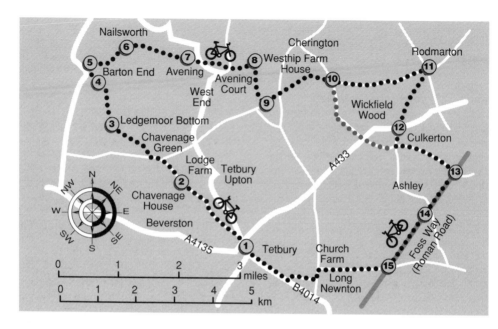

such a short distance in quiet surroundings it's less hassle to turn left along the farm lane for 50yd or so, and then right onto the lane that leads downhill to the main A46.

5. You stay on the A46 for no more than 75yd. As it bears round a fairly tight left-hand bend, cross over to join a narrow dead-end lane on the right, which goes uphill behind a rather fine house. This will lead you eastwards to Avening. Ignore all turn-offs to follow the lane up to a patch of woodland, by which time the tarmac has long disappeared and good bridleway tracks have taken over, which offer plenty of smooth and easy riding.

6. When you come to a ruined barn on the fringes of the woodland, two bridleway signs point left and straight ahead. However, you continue to bear right round the edge of the trees, following the track until you pick up another bridleway sign at the east end of the woods. This directs you onto a rougher track to the left, with about 1¼ miles (2km) to go to Avening.

As you approach this small town the track narrows and drops quite steeply downhill, with a

short but potentially extremely muddy section to snare you before you hit a tarmac lane.

7. Drop steeply downhill to the B4014 on a wrecked tarmac surface. Here you can either turn right to ride into Avening and check out the pub, or if you want to continue straight on, cross over the B4014 and ride up Rectory Lane, which follows the hillside with fine views over the town. Keep riding east along this lane until a 'no entry' sign forces a right turn, sending you down to cross the river bridge. Here you bear left uphill, and then turn right on the road signposted to Cherington.

8. About 500yd (0.5km) out of Avening close to Avening Court the road drops downhill to a patch of white-painted houses by a phone box. Look for a track on the right here, which is bridleway although you don't pick up the bridleway signposts until later. Follow it downhill and uphill, heading south across open fields to the next road junction.

9. At this junction the bridleway goes straight

on and looks inviting, but you turn left, following the lane for 500yd (0.5km) until you cross straight over at the next crossroads. Here you join a bridleway that crosses high ground on fine tracks with about a mile (1.5km) of easy pedalling to a road junction to the south of Cherington.

10. From here you have a choice. Either turn right and follow the road to Culkerton, or go straight on for Rodmarton direct, which offers an interesting bridleway alternative if the conditions are OK. The road that continues east to Rodmarton is mainly an enjoyable, steady, fast downhill ride with trees on either side that are a delight in spring.

11. On the outskirts of Rodmarton turn right towards the A433, and then look out for a signposted bridleway that turns right again to head south-west across the middle of a field. This is lumpy riding when it's dry and would be a horror story if it was wet.

When you reach the Tump Plantation a pleasant section leads across a meadow with another bout of field riding beyond. The problems start when you reach the long line of trees ahead. A dilapidated gate appears to show the way through here, but there's no sign of the bridleway that the OS map shows going straight ahead across the field. Nevertheless that must be the way to go, ignoring the apparent tracks that go round the sides of the field and lead to nothing. If the weather is dry it is OK, with a slight downhill that will bring you to the correct bridleway gate by the side of the A433. The farmer/landowner should of course have left a clear track as required by law, and is to blame if people get lost here.

12. Cross straight over the A433, and follow the narrow lane ahead uphill into Culkerton. From Culkerton follow the road that heads west for Somerford Keynes. After just over ²/₃ mile (1km) you pass New Barn Farm on the right and a strange collection of caravans, and then before the road bears left you come to the ancient Roman Foss Way, which looks pretty inviting in both directions. It would once have extended from

Cirencester, but has now been obliterated north of the Kemble Airfield, which can be seen in the distance.

13. Turn right on the Foss Way, and follow it in a straight line south-west for the next 1³/₄ miles (3km). This should be a lovely ride on a wonderful old road passing through peaceful countryside, but sadly it rates as byway and much of it has been destroyed by the recent use of four wheel drive vehicles, which have carved huge gouges on either side of the track. It seems extraordinary that these things have been allowed to do more damage in a few years than anything else has managed in well over a thousand. How they are allowed to continue to wreck these old roads is beyond belief.

14. Parts of the Foss Way still offer reasonable riding on this section, but do beware of mud! Cross the first road junction at Fosse Gate, and then turn off at the next road. Tetbury is where we are heading for on this route, but another time it would be interesting to explore the Foss Way as it continues its dead straight line to the south-west.

15. Turn right along the road for Tetbury, following it west for about 1¹/₄ miles (2km) to the fine building of Church Farm. Turn left at the T-junction here, and then opposite the lonely church at Long Newnton turn right onto a wide bridleway track that is clearly signposted. After the rigours of the Foss Way this is a lovely offroad section to finish on, but all too soon it bears left and brings you to the B4014. From here it is an easy pedal back into Tetbury.

Places To Visit:
Information Centre at Tetbury
(tel: 01666 503552);
Chavenage House (tel: 01666 502329).

Pubs and Cafés:
Plenty of choice in Tetbury;
pub at Avening.

24 Westonbirt to Wotton

This ride explores the hilly lands to the east of Wotton-under-Edge, where the terrain provides some challenging riding that should not be undertaken lightly. An additional attraction to this ride is that it passes through the grounds of the world-famous Westonbirt Arboretum at the eastern end of the route.

If you like trees, Westonbirt is the place for you. It also makes a good place to start the ride, but remember that parking is not possible inside the grounds unless you pay to go into the arboretum – and from spring to autumn you should be prepared for crowds. Otherwise parking is very limited, though some roadside parking is possible on the A433 or in the hamlet of Westonbirt itself. Alternatively you may prefer to start the ride from Wotton-under-Edge where parking is likely to be rather simpler.

1. Starting from Westonbirt, it's worth a quick tour of the few buildings that make up this hamlet on the south side of the A433, where the grandeur of Westonbirt School contrasts strangely with a most unusual house that is half buried underground.

The bridleway that runs through the grounds of Westonbirt Arboretum starts at the A433 about 100yd south of the main entrance. It follows a deeply sunken track past the back of the Westonbirt Garden Centre, and from there heads straight up the valley with Westonbirt's gardens on either side. If the weather has been wet you will find it very hard going along this section, and you should of course take care to ride slowly past visitors walking around the arboretum.

2. The bridleway is easily followed, leading to a field gate where it leaves the valley of the arboretum to enter Silk Woods. Here the main track that bears to the left is so well churned by horses that it should be a real horror story in wet weather. The track soon emerges from the trees on the west side of Silk Woods, and from here you follow the track straight ahead, heading west on a fairly good surface. Continue through a number of gates until you reach a minor road.

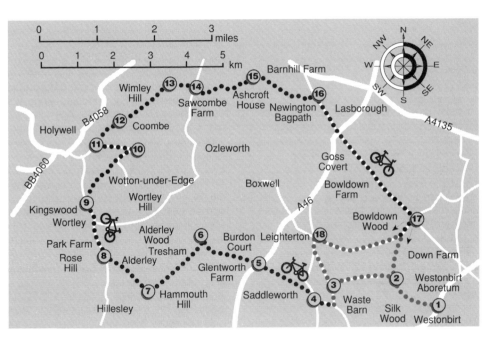

3. Turn left uphill on the road, following it south for about 500yd (0.5km) until you come to a sharp right turn onto a rough track. This gives another stretch of bridleway, heading west for 500yd (0.5km) to the next road junction to the north of Oldbury-on-the-Hill.

4. Turn right on the road here, and then left by the entrance to Saddlewood Manor. On the OS map the bridleway here is shown heading diagonally north-west across the fields, but its route is not easy to follow. If you stray off course there are plenty of lurid and rather unpleasant signs informing you of the penalties of trespass, but they are also patently ridiculous – you have every right to use this bridleway as a short cut to the A46, and there would be no problems if the landowner opted to tell people where to go rather then where not to go.

5. From the bridleway turn left on the A46, and then almost immediately turn right to follow a minor road signposted to Tresham. After a mile (1.5km) the road bears right past the church here,

and then downhill and round to the left where you will see a signposted bridleway going down into the valley.

6. Follow the track downhill from Tresham, heading south-west along the valley bottom with sheep for company. The track is easy to follow and pretty good riding all the way, with a mile (1.5km) under your wheels bringing you to a bridleway junction close to the next road to the north-east of Hillesley.

7. Follow the bridleway right turn through a gate here, to continue north-west along the side of Winner Hill. You start on a narrow track following the hillside, and soon reach the road at the very smart hamlet of Alderley, where you emerge by the side of a fine small manor house with the church opposite.

8. Your next destination is Wortley. The easiest route is to follow the road downhill and across the river. A bridleway option follows a good track to the east, but it then unaccountably turns to footpath and becomes tricky to follow. Follow the road on northwards, and then about 500yd (0.5km) past Wortley look for a signposted bridleway turning off to the right at the top of a small hill.

9. The track here leads steadily uphill on a fairly good surface, following a sunken trail along Little Tor Hill and then breaking out into the open as it heads for the top of Tor Hill.

Keep to the right as you leave the woods, following the tractor-churned track straight up the hillside in a north-east direction. Some of the going is quite hard here and could be especially gruesome in wet weather, but the view from the top is among the best that the Cotswolds can offer, with the Bristol Channel laid at your feet and the mountains of Wales beyond. Keep straight on from the viewpoint until you reach a lane.

10. Ride on along this lane for about 100yd, and then turn sharply left downhill towards Wotton-under-Edge. This is a ferociously steep downhill with woodland on either side, and if you fancy a technical section you may care to slam on the brakes about halfway down and try the bridleway that turns off to the right. This is super steep, fairly narrow and quite rocky near the bottom, and as such is only recommended to those who delight in difficult riding.

11. Turn right at the bottom of the hill to follow the road through to the hamlet of Coombe, crossing a stream and then immediately turning right on a dead-end lane before you start to go uphill on the other side of the valley.

12. Follow this lane as it heads north-east out of Coombe to join a signposted bridleway. From here a good track follows the edge of woodland along the bottom of Wimley Hill, but beware of mud in wet weather. The track breaks out into open ground to follow Tyley Bottom in the same direction through fine valley surroundings, and is quite easy to follow until it narrows and starts to duck and dive through woodland by the side of

a stream, where you will find an abundance of cattle-churned mud to keep you happy.

13. Not before time an easily spotted bridleway post directs you to turn right and head straight up the opposite hillside. More bridleway posts show the way on what soon becomes an unridable slog to the top, but at least the views are good as you battle up to emerge on the road close by a massive radio mast.

14. Turn right and then left on the road here, following a lane that speeds due east. It then drops steeply down into the next valley where you'll find Ashcroft House in the bottom, with an equally steep climb to pull you up the other side.

15. Cross straight over at the next road junction, and then turn right down to Newington Bagpath, where you will pass a rather fine disused church on the hillside. Ride down into the valley, head past the farm, and then zig-zag up the other side to join the road near Lasborough.

16. From here you've got to pedal about 2$\frac{1}{2}$ miles (4km) on a wide, easy road, heading south-east to cross the A46.

17. Past Bowldown Wood, at the foot of a long steady hill, turn right for the village of Leighterton, where the pub awaits. Alternatively, just under $\frac{2}{3}$ mile (1km) along this road you can take the bridleway that turns off southwards to cross into Silk Wood, where it joins the outward route.

18. From Leighterton ride south to rejoin to outward bridleway which can be found near the bottom of a long fast downhill.

Places To Visit:
Westonbirt Arboretum (tel: 01666 880220).

Pubs and Cafés:
Café at Westonbirt Arboretum;
The Royal Oak at Leighterton.

25 Dyrham Park and Tog Hill

This ride explores the countryside to the north of Bath as far as the fringes of Chipping Sodbury, with a visit to the National Trust mansion Dyrham Court thrown in for good measure. For those arriving from Bath there's a convenient start point at Tog Hill on the A420; alternatively start from the car park area just south of Junction 18 of the M4 on the busy A46.

On-Road and Offroad

Area: The southern end of the Cotswolds – a tour of the high and low ground to the north of Bath. Start and finish at the Tog Hill car park on the A420 east of Wick at GR:733727; alternatively start from the M4/A46 car park at GR:756778.

OS Map: Landranger 172 – Bristol, Bath & surrounding area.

Route:
Tog Hill/A420 car park (GR:733727)
Tog Hill/bridleway (GR:726727)
Doynton (GR:720741)
Doynton/bridleway (GR:723749)
M4/bridleway (GR:715778)
Westerleigh Hill/B4465 (GR:707792)
Dodington (GR:749801)
Dodington Ash (GR:758784)
Lower Lapdown Farm/bridleway (GR:768781)
Hinton Hill/bridleway (GR:747766)
M4/A46 car park (GR:756778)
Dyrham (GR:737757)
Doynton/bridleway (GR:723749)
Doynton (GR:720741)
Tog Hill/bridleway (GR:726727)
Tog Hill/A420 car park (GR:733727)

Nearest BR Stations: Yate.

Approx Length: 19 miles (30km).

Nearest Youth Hostel: Bath (tel: 01225 465674)

Time: Allow 3 hours plus stops.

Rating: Rating: Moderate. Some of the bridleway sections are a little frustrating, and could be poor going in wet weather.

1. The Tog Hill car park is conveniently situated to the east of Wick on the A420 at the top of a hill where a famous battle was fought long ago. Ride out of the car park and down the hill, taking it slowly because the bridleway turn-off to the right which will take you north comes after about 500yd (0.5km) at the end of a belt of trees.

2. The bridleway follows a track down by the side of a house and is signposted as a footpath. Nevertheless it is bridleway on the OS map, and you can follow it down a wet and somewhat miserable track which improves as it levels out and leads you to the village of Doynton.

3. Turn left into Doynton, passing the village hall, and then turn right at the T-junction to pass the church, riding out on the Dyrham road. About 2/3 mile (1km) out of Doynton look for a clearly signposted bridleway which crosses the River Boyd at a wooden bridge and is where the main circuit begins.

4. The bridleway follows the River Boyd northwards, and mainly keeps close to its banks. It is fairly easy to follow, crossing grassy meadows on flat land with some mud to be expected in wet weather. After 1 1/4 miles (2km) you come to a lane; keep straight on, and follow the bridleway north until you reach a high-quality crossing track.

5. The OS map shows the bridleway that goes straight ahead here changing into a footpath which is borne out by a stile at the other end, so

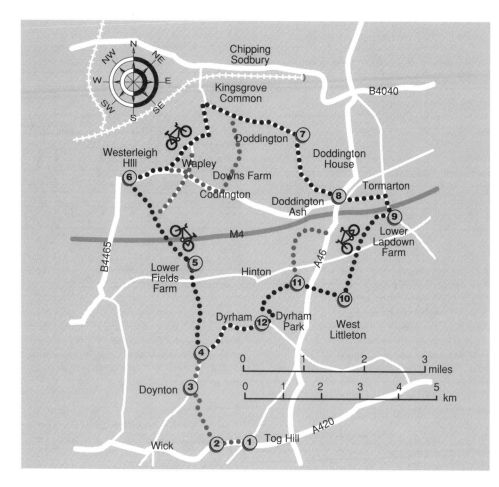

turn left to head north-west along the main track. This rapidly deteriorates as it approaches the M4, with one particularly gruesome section to struggle through. It eventually crosses the M4 on a bridge, joining a much better track that continues through to the B4465 at Westerleigh Hill.

(An option here is to look out for the right-turn bridleway about 500yd (0.5km) north of the M4. This cuts down the distance on-road, emerging north-west of Codrington.)

6. Turn right along the B4465 from Westerleigh. You can then take the second left

turn and follow narrow lanes on a 2¹/₂-mile (4km) northward loop through to Dodington. Alternatively if you ride on as far as the pub in Codrington you'll find a signposted bridleway. This heads north via Downs Farm and Lydes Farm to cut the corner, but is not much fun. Much of the distance follows a narrow, barbed wire fence path by the side of fields that is horribly churned by horses. It's bad enough to push in dry weather, while in the wet it wouldn't bear thinking about! You choose which way to go, but remember that the road route is less stressful.

7. Ride into Dodington, where sadly you are not allowed to follow the private road through the Park. Instead turn right onto the minor road that heads south, with a few dips, dives, twists and turns through pleasant countryside bringing you to Dodington Ash by the entrance to Dodington House, with the complexities of the A46/B4465 interchange ahead of you.

8. Turn left on to the B4465 and cross straight over the A46. Immediately fork right onto a narrow lane, which is part of the Cotswold Way. This leads due east to the outskirts of Tormarton, where a right turn takes you back over the M4.

9. Just south of the M4 a clearly signposted bridleway leads to Lower Lapdown Farm. Follow the bridleway past the farm houses, joining a good track that heads across fields, bearing left towards the nearest electricity pylon – it's important to change course a little here – and coming to a narrow lane after about ²/₃ mile (1km) offroad. Watch the crossing here as cars appear to drive very fast. The next section of bridleway goes straight on ahead, following a hard but bumpy track that leads downhill to the road to the north of West Littleton.

10. Turn right on the road here, and after a steady uphill prepare to cross the busy A46. When you have achieved this ride straight on up a lane on the other side, reaching a right hand bend on the top of Hinton Hill which is on the edge of Dyrham Park after just under 500yd (0.5km). A right turn here will take you north along the Cotswold Way, joining a bridleway that leads into the A46 car park to the immediate south of Junction 18 of the M4.

11. To continue the route go straight ahead down the side of Dyrham Park, joining a bridleway that goes along the side of the high wall that keeps the deer locked into their parkland on the left. This is an enjoyable downhill from the top of Hinton Hill, with nice views and a mainly good riding surface. It eventually brings

A memorial to an ancient battleground marks the top of Tog Hill and the southern end of the Cotswolds.

you to a lane on the outskirts of Dyrham, from where it's worth diverting left to get a fine view of Dyrham Park mansion through its ornamental gates. To find the main entrance, you unfortunately need to ride round to the A46.

12. To continue the route, follow the road out of Dyrham signposted for Doynton. Depending on your start point, either retrace your wheeltracks back to the Tog Hill car park, or go to No. 3 of the route instructions to ride north towards the M4.

Places To Visit:
Dyrham Park
(NT – tel: 01225 891364).

Pubs and Cafés:
The Codrington Arms at Codrington;
The Portcullis or Compass
at Tormarton;
NT café pleasantly situated in the
orangery at Dyrham Park.

Cycling Books from the Crowood Press

Great Cycle Routes – North and South Downs	Jeremy Evans
Great Cycle Routes – Dorset and the New Forest	Jeremy Evans
Great Cycle Routes – Dartmoor and Exmoor	Jeremy Evans
Great Cycle Routes – Wales and the Borders	Jeremy Evans
Great Cycle Routes – Cumbria and North Yorkshire	Jeremy Evans
Great Cycle Routes – The Chilterns and the Ridgeway	Jeremy Evans
50 Mountain Bike Rides	Jeremy Evans
Cycling on Road and Trail	Jeremy Evans
Cycling in France	Tim Hughes
Adventure Mountain Biking	Carlton Reid
Cycle Sport	Peter Konopka
Offroad Adventure Cycling	Jeremy Evans
Touring Bikes	Tony Oliver
Mountain Biking – The Skills of the Game	Paul Skilbeck